Healing the Heart

The Transformational Power of Biblical Heart Imagery

Joseph A. Grassi

PAULIST PRESS
New York/Mahwah

Library of Congress Cataloging-in-Publication Data

Grassi, Joseph A.
    Healing the heart.

    Bibliography: p.
    1. Heart—Biblical teaching. 2. Eidetic imagery. 3. Christian life—Catholic authors. I. Title.
BS680.H416G72   1986   220.6'4   86-25132
ISBN 0-8091-2862-4 (pbk.)

Published by Paulist Press
997 Macarthur Boulevard
Mahwah, New Jersey 07430

Printed and bound in the
United States of America

Contents

In memory of my mother,
Marie Di Nunzio Grassi
who first taught me the heart image

Introduction

Over the past twenty years, some of the most exciting psychological discoveries have taken place in the area of applied imagery. By images I do not mean fleeting mental pictures but deeply seated, vivid, emotionally charged, powerful bundles of energy that have often been called "eidetic images." This recent research has proved that images not only represent our desires, but actually have the power to move us into action to accomplish them. While the biblical authors were not acquainted with the scientific aspects of images, they knew their power from experience and applied them to their teaching and preaching. For example, the prophet Isaiah (2:4) kept repeating to Israel the powerful visionary image of a sword beaten into a plowshare, a symbol that has motivated peacemakers for thousands of years.

The heart is the most influential and dynamic of all human images. This is due to its origins in our formational womb experience for over nine months. In the Bible, the word/image for heart is found close to a thousand times. The purpose of this book is to explore the deep significance of biblical heart language/images. It will also point out important avenues of practical application in teaching, healing and personal transformation. To make the book as effective as possible, we have placed practical exercises and suggestions for application throughout the book. In this way, the healing image of the heart can be a valuable instrument for vibrant and meaningful daily living.

1
The Dynamic Transformational
Power of Images

In essence, what people visualize is what they get. Likewise, what they have is the result of what they have previously visualized.

This is the simple conclusion of Samuels' book, *Seeing With the Mind's Eye.*[1] Human experience is enough to ratify this conclusion. As a simple illustration, everyone knows that golfers who imagine that their next shot will land in a lake set up automatically a negative fear emotion that invariably accomplishes what is least wanted. I am reminded of a recent newspaper cartoon of a president of a pessimist society addressing the assembled members with these words, "Congratulations. Our worst fears have been realized."

On the positive side, it has long been accepted and proved by experiments that an image of success not only gives confidence, but actually has within it the power to bring about the desired effect. For example, skilled basketball players see their shot already in the basket before it leaves the hand. It has been demonstrated that the combination of imagination with drills is an important key to progress not only in athletics but in any skill that involves body and mind coordination.

Extending this even further, human experience indicates that strong positive images send out energy and vibrations that seem to draw out the desired effects as if by a hidden magnetism. Jesus himself provided an example of the powerful influence of an image in connection with prayer when he said,

> Have faith in God. Truly, I say to you, whoever says to this mountain, "Be taken up and cast into the sea," and does not doubt in his heart, but believes that whatever is said will come to pass, it will be done for him. Therefore I tell you, whatever you ask in prayer, believe that you have received it, and you will (Mk 11:22–24).

In this passage, "the mountain uprooted and cast into the sea" represents a seemingly impossible effect. However, the secret of success lies in imagining it already obtained through unlimited confidence in God's power in accord with Jesus' words not to doubt in the *heart* but to "believe that whatever is said will come to pass." The repetition in the expression "believe that you have received it" (the Greek past tense) is meant to confirm the surprising statement. St. Paul probably has in mind Jesus' words when he writes about the "faith that removes mountains" (1 Cor 13:2).

Anthropological studies show that human beings for hundreds of thousands of years have accepted the innate power of images and used them effectively in their daily lives. Ancient cave drawings of hunted animals have been found that go back to the dawn of history. Many of these pictures show obvious signs of puncture by spears and other weapons. This demonstrates the ancient belief that power over the image means power over what it represents. Examples of such ancient cave drawings are found in the subterranean caves of Altamura in northern Spain. They have often been called "the Sistine Chapel" of the prehistoric world. On the ceilings are sketches of horses, bisons, wild boars and other hunted animals. Another famous grotto is that of Lascaux in France. The use of animal masks likewise goes back many thousands of years. These were put on before the hunt and worn during rituals, dancing and prayers to insure success. Participants were convinced that identification with animal images meant actual control and power over them in daily life.

These images were actually ways of becoming part of the animal world. Images made it possible for early man and woman to become one with the universe around them—animals, birds, fish, plants, trees. It was the one common Spirit that gave life to all. Carl Jung relates the statement made to him by a Pueblo Indian chief.

> We are a people who live on the roof of the world; we
> are the sons of Father Sun, and with our religion, we
> daily help our father to go across the sky.[2]

Thus the rituals and imagery they used were ways to renew and draw energy from this relationship. So the Indian chief added, "We do this not only for ourselves, but for the whole world. If we were to cease practicing our religion, in ten years the sun would no longer rise."

Ancient images such as these lie at the origins of words, which are actually ways to evoke specific images that we need. Words in turn create language, which is the unique way we have to relate to one another and the world around us. Language has an innate power within it because of the powerful images which it is able to evoke. However, as Samuels[3] has pointed out, as language developed, words were not only used to evoke images, but to separate one's self from the experiences and to categorize them. In time, this resulted in the function of the word as a separator becoming more important than its sensation sharing role. Perception became a matter of identifying objects in terms of labels. All of this points to the essential need to recover the primary use of images and symbols if we are to have a deep relationship to the world around us.

It is especially the healing professions that have effectively used the power of imagery over the centuries. In Egypt, Hermes believed in the intimate connection between mind and world. He taught his followers that the way to cure disease was to imagine perfect states of health in the mind, which would produce the desired effect in the body. Some ancient Greek healers instructed their patients to dream that the gods came to cure them. To provide the necessary atmosphere for this, the Greeks had many temples or shrines for healing. Patients often came from a long distance and stayed at the shrine for the healing process. This started with a bath and a purifying diet as well as fasting. The healing god's image was then applied to the disease-affected parts of the body. The patients were then brought into special temple rooms to sleep. There they awaited dreams from the healing gods along with images of their cure, or instructions about how to proceed with needed remedies. Thus we see how important the image of the healer was in bringing about the desired cure. A similar process was used by Mary Baker Eddy, who founded the Christian Science movement in the nineteenth century. She taught that all disease was caused by the human mind; healing, wholeness and health were in the divine mind. The way to restoration was to bring the divine mind and its image of health into the human mind.

In recent years, a number of physicians have achieved notable results using images in the healing process. For example, Dr. Carl Simington,[4] a radiology cancer specialist, has achieved considerable success in teaching visualization techniques to cancer patients. By careful observation, he noticed that some patients who had been classified as "terminally ill" had "miraculously" recovered despite all unfavorable medical prognosis. He noted that those who did recover had positive attitudes toward life that were reinforced by corresponding images. This demonstrated for him the power of mind images over bodily health. As a result, he decided to apply this process toward healing patients with cancer. They were instructed to imagine the white blood cells as a victorious army marching into battle with malignant cancer cells, destroying them and carrying them out of the body. Follow-up tests showed that all patients who carefully followed instructions had a dramatic improvement.

It is important to keep in mind that images are not an interesting "extra" but are intimately connected with our nature as human beings and the way that we function. All our knowledge comes to us through our organs of perception— eyes, ears, nose, taste and touch. Taking an example, suppose we see a house at a distance. Rays of reflected light bring a representation of this house to our eyes. The cornea and lens focus the rays to form an object on the eye retina. From there, our optic nerves convey a message to the brain's visual area that patterns of light have been received by the eye. Then these are interpreted by the brain which forms an unconscious image that *represents* the house, but is not an actual visual picture. The unconscious image must be decoded for us to form an actual visual image of the house in our imagination.

The distinction between unconscious and conscious image is significant. For example, a heart image need not be a "Valentine" picture or an anatomical heart. The unconscious image of the heart includes much more than this. It is

packed with energy that comes from bodily sensations, emotions and feelings that have come from many sources in our
experience. Tremendous amounts of hidden power may be
locked into unconscious images. These unconscious as well
as conscious images are stored permanently within us. They
become available in memory, dreams, fancy and imagination. Sometimes the unconscious images contain so much
threatening matter that they are hidden and locked within until a favorable time or situation allows them to be recovered
and healed.

The imagination process has many important conse-
quences for us. Bodily reactions and emotions can come just
as forcibly and sometimes even more so from an inner image
of an object/person than from the actual perception in reality
outside. An imagined unpleasant situation such as a painful
tooth removal can bring tears to our eyes and deep emotions
of fear even though no dentist or diseased tooth is present.
The actual image contains the power much more than the object it represents. An example of this, in regard to the heart,
shows how this can happen. Samuels[5] relates the experiment
of A.R. Luria who made use of strong images to change his
heart pulse from seventy beats per minute to one hundred
and then back again. The image used was that of arriving
late at a railroad platform and running faster and faster to
catch up with the last coach of a train just pulling out of the
station. The reverse was accomplished by the image of lying
in bed and gradually falling asleep with breathing becoming
longer and the heart beating slower. Thus images have
within themselves the power to affect and change bodily reactions, even in the heart.

By way of summary and application to the chapters that
follow, we may state the following:

1. Our whole direction of personal growth has been profoundly influenced by powerful inner emotion-packed im-

ages. Any significant personal change must be through some kind of transformation or healing of these images.

2. To set in motion a course of action, we form an image first, or draw on previously recorded images. *The power within these images is enough to bring any action to completion.* Thus the will has a tremendous indirect power, in regard to the images it can summon, or help to form. The will can also act directly and coercively. This can achieve important short term results. However, in the long run, such direct coercive use will prove harmful and self-defeating. The will can skillfully select images, but cannot go directly against them except briefly and at the cost of great violence and bodily harm. Hence the importance of the development of a *skillful* will as emphasized by Assagioli[6] in his books, *Psychosynthesis* and *The Act of the Will*. The careful use of images is the key to personal and spiritual growth.

3. This careful use of images in personal growth is especially true of what are called *eidetic* images. These are especially vivid and emotionally packed images formed during childhood or times of crisis. In the next chapter we will see that the heart image is our most powerful eidetic image that begins to form in early embryonic existence, continues during the nine months in the womb, and even outside the womb especially during the first years of life. This means that the most dramatic and effective influences on personal growth come about through eidetic images, especially the biblical heart image.

2
The Roots of Revelation:
God, the Womb and the Heart

The power, energy, and origins of the biblical heart image go back to God and the unique way he acts in human beings. The Bible describes God as the source of limitless, infinite energy. We find this image in the story of the revelation of God's name to Moses at Sinai. Moses had been forced to flee Egypt because of his violent defense of an abused, beaten Hebrew slave. He then became a shepherd in Sinai, tending the flocks of Jethro, his father-in-law. One day during his wanderings, he came across a most unusual sight: a bush burning with fire, and yet not being consumed. He said to himself, "I will turn aside and see this great sight, why the bush is not burnt" (Ex 3:3).

Within this burning bush God revealed to Moses who he was. He was not a distant divinity, but one who worked in and through people. He said to Moses, "I am the God of your father, the God of Abraham, the God of Isaac, and the God of Jacob" (3:6). In other words, Moses was not to look for some far-off god, but one who even lived and worked in his own father and mother, and whose activity extended as far as Abraham, Isaac and Jacob, the great patriarchs. When Moses asked for God's name, he only responded, "I AM

10

WHO AM" (3:14). By this response, God removed himself from the category of divinities whose revealed names gave people a measure of control over them, perhaps even magical. To the contrary, the Hebrew God was the supremely uncontrollable. He could not be used or "burnt-out" because he was the burning bush never consumed, the source of limitless energy.

This category of limitless energy provides a valuable key to the Hebrew understanding of God. Today, every schoolchild soon learns Einstein's famous equation: E equals MC^2—that energy is convertible with matter. We are living in a nuclear age, where it is commonplace knowledge that even a teaspoon of water contains an unbelievable reservoir of energy locked up within the hydrogen and oxygen atoms. For us, this is mainly an intellectual matter obtained from textbooks, as well as from information about nuclear power stations and even nuclear warheads. However, the ancients experienced in their whole beings what we sometimes know only with our minds. They lived in a universe of felt energy vibrations and they knew that God was the source of this unseen power. They believed that God communicated this energy to human beings in a very unique way in the creation and birth process.

Accordingly, to understand the dynamic power of the heart image, we must go to the origins of each human life. The biblical appreciation of this was based on the psychological experience of every human child during the first nine months of its existence. In the dark waterbed of the womb, there were two dominant rhythms, those of mother's breathing and heartbeat. The watery envelope within the womb compressed or expanded as she breathed, and this movement shook and moved the embryo. Between the two rhythms of breath and heartbeat we led a "rock and roll" existence long before our feet could move or dance.

The second heartbeat rhythm was intimately connected with the first breathing rhythm. It was connected because the air that mother breathed came into her blood in the form of life-giving oxygen that was brought into the fetus through the life-line of the umbilical cord. While the ancients did not know the scientific components of air, they were keenly aware that blood was the bearer and transmitter of life, and that the central transfer point was the heart. The Hebrew conviction of the holiness of blood was built on this appreciation and the realization that this life in the blood came directly from the Creator.

This second heart-beat rhythm is responsible for the powerful heart image that penetrates our whole human existence. This can be illustrated by some observations. Our first nine months were dominated by the incessant maternal heart-throb. This beat was a total experience as each pulsating movement of the umbilical cord shook us in the watery capsule of the womb. It is staggering to try to imagine the total psychological effect of this maternal heart-beat averaging 60 a minute, 3,600 an hour, 86,400 a day and close to twenty-four million during the time of gestation. In the womb, we could sense times of rest when mother went to sleep and her heart-beat slowed to 40–50 beats a minute, and then we rested also. There were times when the rhythm speeded up during times of exercise or excitement. Then we became excited also and moved around more than usual. During all this time, a most powerful eidetic image of the heart began to form.

The deep emotional effect of mother's heart-beat did not stop after birth but continued on for months afterward through the hours of nursing each day. The infant, pressed against the mother's breast, was able to keenly sense this beat and prolong the womb experience. Studies[7] have shown a pronounced preference (by mother and child) to the left breast because the heart-beat was sensed most strongly in this position. Tests[8] have even demonstrated that infants exposed to the sound of a human heart outside the time of nursing cry less and gain weight faster. In fact, mother's heart-beat has even been commercialized by companies that will sell a maternal heart-beat simulator for under baby's pillow (for $49.95). The guarantee states that baby will cry less, gain weight more rapidly, etc. A nurse recently told me of an old "secret" used by nurses years ago: placing alarm clocks under pillows to achieve the same effect through the loud ticking. It seems that instinct precedes scientific studies.

Since the roots of the heart image lie in the womb experience, it is essentially a feminine image. The womb sensations were mostly tactile, but they became auditory when the infant nursed at mother's breasts. The breasts became a continuation of the womb existence. The liquid nourishment was still primary as mother's milk took the place of the blood once transferred directly from her heart. In addition, the first visual image of the child was the mother's breast from which life itself proceeded along with the continuation of the reassuring womb heart-beat. The woman's breast thus became a dominant visual image that would go through all of life. In the Bible this is witnessed by the frequent association of womb and breasts. Jacob, for example, called down upon his family the blessings of womb and breast (Gen 49:25).

These two great rhythms of existence were intimately connected with God. In regard to the first, we find mention of the spirit or breath of God right from the first pages of the Bible and over a thousand times throughout. This breath/ spirit was linked to the continuous communication and sharing of divine energy within the universe. The wind/air was considered the bearer of this energy and the breathing process was its mode of communication. Once again, biblical men and women knew that breathing was essentially an energy process. The first pages of Genesis point to God as the source and communicator of this energy. The creation of man and woman is described in this way:

> Then the Lord God formed man of the dust from the ground, and breathed into his nostrils the breath of life; and man became a living being (2:7).

The Hebrew word for spirit is *ruach* which is almost synonymous with breath, wind and life. A prime characteristic of life is breathing since animals and human beings die when they stop breathing. This life-breath is something mysterious and alien to us. We do not possess or control it. It comes as a gift at birth and departs usually unexpectedly, despite all our will and efforts. We can control our breathing for brief moments when aware of it, but most of the time, especially at night, it goes on without our conscious control. The ancients thought of this life-breath as a share in the divine energy and life that fills all the world It comes into human beings at birth and returns to its source at death. Death is a removal of this spirit in Genesis 6:3 where God speaks about the limitation of human life in these words, "My spirit shall not abide in man forever, for he is flesh, but his days shall be a hundred and twenty years."

The frequent mention of spirit/breath in the Bible tells us that the writers were very much aware of their breath and breathing process. This awareness bcame an important way to remember God's presence and draw strength from it. It is quite remarkable that the prophet Elisha almost three thousand years ago recognized the tremendous energy process in breathing. He restored a young man to life by placing his own mouth on the mouth of the boy and breathing into his mouth until he revived (2 Kgs 4:34). We recognize here a mouth-to-mouth resuscitation technique that was only re-introduced within the last few decades.

The connection between breath, wind and the life-giving action of God is found in a very dramatic fashion in Ezekiel 37. The prophet was carried in a vision to a great valley filled with dry bones. God asked him whether it was possible for these bones to come to life. He then ordered Ezekiel to prophesy with these words:

> Prophesy to the breath (spirit); prophesy, son of man, and say to the breath, "Thus says the Lord God: Come from the four winds, O breath, and breathe upon these slain, that they may live." I prophesied as he commanded me, and the breath came into them, and they lived, and stood upon their feet, an exceedingly great host (37:9–10).

Related to the creation and Ezekiel texts, we find the same awareness of breath/spirit and its divine origin in the New Testament. After his resurrection, Jesus appears to the twelve and breathes upon them, communicating the Holy Spirit/Breath of God: "And when he had said this, he (Jesus) breathed upon them and said to them, 'Receive the Holy Spirit' " (Jn 20:22).

In regard to the second rhythm, the maternal heartbeat in the womb, God's mysterious action was considered to be centered here in the whole birth process. The psalmist praises God in these words, "You did form my inmost parts; you knit me together in my mother's womb" (138: 13). The Book of Job describes the womb as the special locus of God's creative activity: "Did not he who made me in the womb make him? And did not one fashion us in the womb?" (31:15). This action in the womb is so primary to God's nature that the word *rechem,* (Hebrew, womb) is at the root of the word *rachum,* meaning "merciful" or "compassionate" that is used to describe the very essence of God. This description is found in the unusual story in Exodus 33:18–34:7 where Moses daringly asked for a vision of God's glory. God answers that no human being can see him and continue to live. However, God allows Moses to hide in the hollow of a rock as he passes by and pronounces his great name:

> The Lord passed before him, and proclaimed, "The Lord, the Lord, a God merciful and gracious, slow to anger and abounding in steadfast love and faithfulness" (34:5–6).

The first word used is "merciful," *rachum,* from the root *rechem,* or womb. It is most significant that to describe God's very essence, the feminine and maternal aspect is needed, since it is a human being's primal experience of love and care. It is this quality that is the root cause of revelation. It is characterized by a deep listening and openness to all of creation, especially the needs of human beings. In the burning bush at Sinai, God said:

> I have seen the affliction of my people who are in Egypt, and have heard their cry because of their taskmasters; I know their sufferings, and I have come down to deliver them out of the hand of the Egyptians (Ex 3:7–8).

The triple expression "seeing, hearing and knowing" emphasizes the qualities of listening and mercy. This is what prompts God to become a liberator for his people. In Hebrew this beautiful quality is described as a "listening heart."

This biblical way of describing God's nature has a profound effect on social ethics and justice. These latter are not extras or optional responses to God, but flow directly from the God's essence. Just as God first moved to liberate his people through this quality of a "listening heart," so human beings created to God's image must necessarily respond in the same way to liberate the poor and oppressed wherever they may be. This is the foundation of a true "liberation theology." The Gospel of Luke echoes this in the parable of the Good Samaritan (11:28–37) who responded to the stranger lying on the road not because of any legal obligation but because he was "moved to compassion." The Greek has *esplagchnisthē,* meaning literally a "gut reaction." While some might call this a "humanistic" response, the Bible sees it as a gift of God's own *rachum* or womb compassion.

Summary

The two fundamental life rhythms are breath/spirit, beginning from the womb, and the maternal heart-beat proceeding along the pulsating umbilical cord. These have far-reaching effects as the images of all love, harmony, music, and rhythm in the world. In the Bible, they are both inseparable from God, whose spirit or breath is the source of all life. This life is found in the blood as propelled by each pulsation of the heart. God's action in the womb is so profound that his great name revealed to Moses is that of *Rachum,* the merciful one, coming from the root *rechem* meaning the womb. This source of compassion, love and mercy prompts God to listen to the sufferings of his people in Egypt and come down to save them. It is also the fountain and source of all mercy, love and justice between human beings on earth.

Exercises and Application

In this book we are concerned not only with intellectual knowledge, but with felt experience. Consequently, we will have some suggested exercises to help promote more conscious awareness of the power of heart images. These can provide us with new energies for daily life as we apply the most powerful symbols of human existence to the process of personal growth.

1. We have seen that the biblical peoples had a deep awareness of breath and the breath/energy process. They felt that this was their essential link with God the source of all energy and the spirit/breath of the universe. In addition, all the great world religions have attached great importance to breathing awareness in meditation and prayer. In our modern world, this consciousness becomes easily lost. The following are some hints:

◊ Start off by just observing your breath, being careful not to control it. Using a watch, count how many breaths you take in a minute.
◊ Take frequent "breathers" during the day when you can just be aware of and enjoy your breathing. Even a traffic stop can afford a wonderful opportunity as so many others grind their teeth.
◊ Move to a deeper appreciation of your breath as participation in the great energy of the universe. As you breathe in, say to yourself, "Come, Holy Spirit." As you breathe out, send that energy to some particular need in your own life or that of others.

2. Begin to be more aware of the heart-beat rhythm in your body.

◇ Continue the previous breathing exercise but be especially aware of the little space between breaths. This space is quite evident at night when we observe another person's breathing (where the interval can be quite long). As you do this concentrate on the region of your heart. Gradually, you will detect your heart-beat at the "quiet times" between respiration.

◇ As you become proficient, unite your heart-beat to that of others—family, loved ones, etc.—in a gradually extending fashion. Then feel God working in all these hearts as the great, loving, compassionate, energy-filled heart-beat of the universe, where even the smallest atoms have their own "beat" and rhythm. Absorb as much energy and warmth as you can from these images, and bring it into important areas and situations of your own life.

3. We have noted the primal feminine aspect of God in his *rachum,* womb compassion, from *rechem,* womb. Yet we constantly pray to God as "Father." It would be more in accord with God's revelation of his name to pray to "Our Father and Mother" or to alternate between Father and Mother in accord with the masculine and feminine sides of God that manifest themselves. Unfortunately, male images of power have dominated our concept of the Hebrew-Christian God. This has caused a relative neglect of the female images, especially the most primal maternal image of God working in the womb. The constant use of "he" in reference to God tends to reinforce male, patriarchal images of God.

3
Biblical Heart Language
and Heartless Technology

The language of the Bible is literally heart language. The word for heart is found over a thousand times, about 850 in the Old Testament and 150 in the New Testament. For the Hebrews, the heart was not only the source of feelings, desires and thoughts, but also the very center of the spirit's activities in each person. This view came from their holistic view of the human body. The ears, the eyes, the mouth, the heart, etc., are all mysteriously interconnected so that people can "listen with their hearts," or even speak directly to another person's heart. The English language still retains much of this view. The Oxford Dictionary of the English Language has fifty-six categories of meaning under "heart," making it one of the most "loaded" words in the English language. Only four of these categories concern the actual physical organ. The remainder deal with metaphoric meanings, e.g., "to break one's heart," "to lose heart," "heart to heart," and hundreds of others.

The nineteenth and the first part of the twentieth centuries dealt a mortal blow to this holistic view of the heart and the human person. Mechanistic views of the human body presented it as a conglomeration of separate organs joined together for a common purpose. In this view, the brain was like a telephone switchboard of the whole apparatus: the heart was a pump to keep the blood moving, the eyes were like the camera, the lungs were the bellows, etc. Scientific findings of the later twentieth century reversed this false view. It is now recognized that both the brain and the heart are interconnected with every cell in the human body. Thus we have intellectually recovered what the ancients knew in a very feeling way: our somatic oneness with the heart as a special centering place because of the conflux of nerves and interchange of blood and vitality at this point. However, the healing sciences, medicine and religion have only slowly recovered from the terrible setback of previous mechanistic views of the whole person.

With this holistic view in mind, it is significant that the Hebrew scriptures are written in essentially "heart language." By this I mean that the heart appears as the center of feelings, will, desires, thoughts, remembering, and relationships. It is also the central place of God's action in human beings. Some examples from each of these categories will be helpful. (It should be noted that the original "heart" in the Hebrew has disappeared in some English translations which either paraphrase it or use "mind" or "understanding" instead.)

Feelings

The heart can be joyful: "My heart is glad, and my soul rejoices" (Ps 16:9). It can sing (Job 29:13). The heart can cry in sorrow (Lam 2:18) or be faint so the whole body weakens (Deut 20:3). It can feel grief (Gen 6:6), tremble (1 Sam 4:13), or be broken (Ps 51:17). It can be proud, or lifted up (Deut 8:14). In contrast, it may be humble (Lev 26:41). Either love (Deut 6:5) or hatred (Lev 19:17) can fill it. It can be like a burning fire (Jer 20:9) or envious (Prov 23:17).

Will

Jonathan's armor-bearer tells him, "Do whatever is in your heart" (1 Sam 14:7). The plans of the heart belong to man (Prov 21:2). The prophet Samuel said to the people, "If you wish to turn to the Lord with your whole heart . . ." (1 Sam 7:3).

Desires

It is very hard to distinguish between will and desires since they are so intermingled. The heart can move in various directions in regard to desires. The psalmist can sing that God has given him his heart's desire (21:2). Love for another person can be expressed as "setting a seal on the heart" (Cant 8:6). In the opposite direction, someone who looks at a woman with lust in his heart has already committed adultery with her" (Mt 5:28). Thus the heart can move in various directions or waver back and forth: a person can have a "double heart" (1 Chr 12:33; Ps 12:2).

This ambivalence of the heart is an important biblical theme. The heart can desire or will good or evil. However it seems to tend more toward evil without God's special help and inspiration. Dr. Jo Milgrom[9] calls this an "ambivalent creative power" of the heart. She notes that after Abel's murder, the corruption of the flood, and the seduction of the sons of God, God remarks, "The tendency (ambivalent creative power) of man's heart is evil from its youth" (Gen 8:21). On the other side, God can heal the heart and turn the whole direction of man toward God's love and service. Thus, at the end of the First Book of Chronicles, David prays,

Grant to Solomon my son that with a whole heart he may keep thy commandments, thy testimonies, and thy statutes, performing all, and that he may build the palace for which I have made provision (29:19).

A heart such as this, healed and turned to God, is called a whole or perfect heart from the Hebrew root *shalom,* meaning peace. So David addresses his son Solomon:

And you, Solomon my son, know the God of your father and serve him with a whole heart and with a willing mind: for the Lord searches all hearts, and understands every plan and thought. If you seek him, he will be found by you; but if you forsake him, he will cast you off forever (1 Chr 28:9).

Thoughts

To think is to speak to one's self within the heart as in Ecclesiastes 1:16, "I spoke with my heart." It is interesting that the rabbinic midrash on this text proceeds by giving some sixty examples of heart language with various meanings. The heart understands. Solomon prays to God, "Give your servant a listening heart" (1 Kgs 3:9). It meditates: "The meditation of my heart shall be understanding" (Ps 49:3).

Remembering

To remember is to "call to heart" (Jer 19:5). The teacher in Proverbs tells his "son" to write his words on the tablets of the heart (3:3).

The Special Place of God's Action and Repentance

Only God can create a "clean heart," so the psalmist prays, "Create in me a clean heart" (51:10). God "enlarges the heart" so it can have true wisdom (Ps 119:32). He puts wisdom in the heart of Solomon (1 Kgs 10:24). God gave King Saul "another heart" (1 Sam 10:9). King Josiah "turned to the Lord with all his heart and with all his soul, and with all his might" (2 Kgs 23:25). The prophet Malachi announces that Elijah will return before the great day of the Lord to turn the hearts of fathers toward their children, and children toward their fathers" (4:4–5). Only God can change stony hearts into hearts of flesh to keep his commandments (Ez 36:26). God alone sees the condition of the human heart. True knowledge of God is God's special gift: "I will give them a heart to know that I am the Lord" (Jer 24:7). A true conversion is to return to God with the whole heart and not in pretense (Jer 3:10; 29:13).

Relationships and Agreement

When King Jehu decided to begin a return of Israel to the religion of Yahweh, he asked Jehonadab, "Is your heart true to my heart as mine is to yours?" (2 Kgs 10:15). To request a deep relationship between teacher and student, the author of Proverbs writes, "My son, give me your heart" (23:26). True intimacy is to speak directly to a person's heart. So Boaz spoke to Ruth (Ru 2:13) and so God speaks to Israel (Is 40:2). Samson told Delilah all that was in his heart (Jgs 16:18).

Unity

All of Israel was of a single heart to make David the king (1 Chr 12:38). "The hand of God was also upon Judah to give them one heart to do what the king and the princes commanded by the word of the Lord" (2 Chr 30:12). In the New Testament the Acts of the Apostles notes that "the company of those who believed were of one heart and soul." This prompted them even to sell houses and property to aid the poor (4:32).

While we have categorized various uses of the heart in the Bible, it should be remembered that they are not separate in action. Emotion and feelings accompany will, thoughts, desires, repentance and memory. This means that we are dealing with a holistic view of the human person and the total direction of a person's existence.

Notes on the Significance of Biblical Heart Language

The heart language of the Bible is in the process of gradually being lost. Many translations either omit entirely the word found in the original text, or substitute "mind" or other equivalents. To gauge the effects of this, we must see how this affects our language. Human language has two main components: (1) the original emotional or tribal function, some of which is shared by animals, who are well able to express their feelings (heart language gives full attention to this component); (2) information or factual exchange, which is the speciality of human beings. However, with the unprecedented explosion of knowledge in the last decades, this last type of language is gradually crowding out the most ancient tribal component. Aiding in this process are computers which are gradually taking over. Home and desk computer sales now dominate the consumer market. Within a few years it will even be considered a "necessity" to own and carry a personal computer. It is shocking to think that most of the ingredients needed to start a nuclear war are handled by computers without the language component of feeling that could alone prevent such wars.

This massive influx of informational "computer type" language has had profound effects on our language, our culture and even our health. Millions of people spend most of their daily work time using this type of language. Consequently, emotional or heart language has become more and more suppressed. This results in increasing stress in the modern technological world. Studies[10] have demonstrated the connection between this stress and heart illnesses. This is because the suppression of heart language results in suppression and constriction of the heart itself. Excessive concentration on informational "computer type" language means that we are effectively telling the heart not to beat and to hold back.[11]

By way of healing contrast, biblical heart language is fully emotional as well as informational language. In addition to the examples already provided, we may note that the Old Testament uses the emphatic personal pronoun "I" only six or seven times. Feelings are expressed in terms of the heart: e.g., "my heart is heavy, joyful, warm, sad, etc." This mode of expression is based on a total view of the human person which modern science is now gradually recovering. Biblical heart language helps us to recover this holistic viewpoint.

All this is especially relevant to religion and theology. These should never overstress the content or informational elements to the detriment of heart language if it is to be faithful to the Bible. It should be kept in mind that the same language used of men and women in the Bible is also used in reference to God without stress on philosophical abstractions. An excessive concentration on informational or "computer type" language can kill the essential affective element in genuine religion. In contrast, biblical heart language totally involves the human person in a meaningful relationship to God and human beings that is supported by feelings and sensitivity.

Summary

Biblical language is characterized by a very prominent use of heart imagery coming from a holistic view of the human person. The heart appears as the center of feelings, will, desires, thoughts, remembering and agreements. It is the center of God's activity in the human person to bring about change, repentance and renewal. Heart language with its full emotional and tribal component is gradually becoming lost in modern technological society with disastrous results to language itself, culture and even health. Restoration of heart language is essential for the recovery of holistic living. This is especially true of the areas of religion and theology.

Exercise and Practice

In the survey of biblical heart language, we found that only divine action could enable the human heart to become a vessel of God's love. We can now deal more directly with heart imagery. Continue the breathing exercise in Chapter 1 as follows:

As you breathe in, say to yourself, "Come, Holy Spirit," as before. As you breathe out, focus on your heart and add, "Fill our hearts with love." This is adapted from Romans 5:5, where Paul writes that the love of God is poured into our hearts by the Holy Spirit who is given us. Repeat this often, experiencing fully God's warmth and energy filling your heart. To intensify the results, use an accompanying *mudra* (bodily movement) as well: lift up your hands and form them into a receptive cup as you breathe in and recite "Come, Holy Spirit." Imagine you are receiving the divine gift of love in your hands. Then bring your hands down and press them on your heart region as you say, "Fill our hearts with love." Do this especially in the morning and evening to bring new energy and love into each day. If there is some person or situation to which you wish to direct that loving energy, end the gesture by spreading out your hands as if in that direction.

4
The Secret of Wisdom:
The Listening Heart

In Chapter 1 we found that God's wombal quality of compassion, *rachum,* prompted him to listen, to feel and experience the sufferings of his people in Egypt, and then to intervene in their behalf. God's supreme quality is that of a compassionate listener to his people. In imitation, the highest quality a human being can attain is to be like God in this sensitive, listening capacity.

In Hebrew, this quality has its source in a "listening heart." This is beautifully described in the stories about King Solomon, who is presented during his youth as a patron and model of wisdom (1 Kgs 3–5). On one occasion during a feast, he offered in prayer a thousand holocausts, symbolic of his desire to devote himself completely to God. That night he had a dream in which God said to him, "Ask whatever you wish and I will give it to you." Solomon's greatest desire was to serve God's people, so he replied, "Give your servant an understanding heart to govern your people, that I may discern between good and evil, for who is able to govern this your great people?" (3:9). The phrase "understanding heart" is literally in Hebrew a "listening heart." Only this quality can make the king like God in his supreme quality of listener to his people. It is so much a divine characteristic that only God can bestow it as a special gift in response to prayer.

For this reason the text makes special note of God's gift of wisdom to the young Solomon: "I now do according to your word. Behold I give you a wise and understanding heart so that none like you has been before you" (3:12). This gift of a "listening heart" enables Solomon to have a deep openness and sensitivity to his people so he can make wise decisions for their benefit.

To illustrate this gift of a "listening heart," the biblical author narrates the story of an "impossible case" of two prostitutes who came to Solomon for judgment. The two lived together and each had a newly-born child. One child, however, died during the night, and each mother claimed the living child as her own. These two women were the only witnesses. Solomon's solution is based on the inner sensitivity of a listening heart. He pretends to threaten to have a soldier divide the child in half with a sword to solve the problem. After carefully noticing which woman is more visibly affected by this threat, Solomon orders the child to be restored to its rightful mother (3:16–18).

This listening heart enables Solomon, the image of the wise person, to be a keen and sensitive observer of all the universe around him: "He spoke of trees, from the cedar that is in Lebanon to the hyssop that grows out of the wall; he spoke also of beasts, and of birds, and of reptiles, and of fish" (4:33). This extraordinary gift of wisdom prompted people to come from everywhere in order to listen to him (4:34).

Another image, that of enlarging the heart, also symbolizes wisdom and brings out the inherent divine gift:

> And God gave Solomon wisdom and understanding be-
> yond measure and largeness of heart like the sand on the

seashore, so that Solomon's wisdom surpassed the wisdom of all the people of the east, and all the wisdom of Egypt (4:29–30).

The English dictionary retains the similar metaphor of such a person as being "open-hearted." The Bible also uses the heart image in relation to sensitive language addressed to another person, e.g., "he spoke to her heart" (Jgs 19:3). This type of speech results in a corresponding response "from the heart."

In direct opposition to a listening heart is a hard, insensitive heart or a "heart of stone." In Egypt, God had listened to his people and had come down to help them. In contrast, the pharaoh's heart was *hard* (Ex 7:13, 22, etc.). He refused to listen to Moses and only increased the people's burdens. The prophet Ezekiel refers to a heart of stone as typical of those who are not open to obedience to God. Only the Spirit can change these hearts into sensitive hearts of flesh so they will be true, obedient children of God (36:26). In the Book of Daniel, the sensitive listening heart is so fundamental to human nature that the lack of it makes a person a beast. Consequently, to picture the lowest state to which a person can fall, the punishment of the Babylonian king Nebuchadnezzar is that of having his heart changed into that of a beast (4:16).

Summary

The biblical roots of revelation lie in God's supreme listening quality, which finds its ultimate expression in the revelation of his *rachum* or mercy derived from the *rechem* or womb. For human beings, to be like God means to have wisdom in the form of a listening heart. This is illustrated in the story of the young King Solomon. Such a heart is a pure gift from God, and is entirely opposite to a hard heart or a heart of stone which human beings often demonstrate without the special help of God.

Exercise and Practice

Like Solomon, we need to ask for God's greatest gift of a listening heart. This enabled the young king to make difficult decisions as he listened to the deep feelings of his people, especially in the example of the two mothers who came to him for judgment. In today's technological and computer world, it is easy to get in the habit of listening only for facts and information. Boredom comes quickly if these are soon exhausted.

In conversations, practice listening for and sensing the feelings of others. Then feed back to them your understanding on this sensitive level. Conversations will soon enliven as we regain the ability to integrate facts and information with the deep feelings that are sometimes underneath them.

A Recipe for Passionate Living:
The Art of Remembering

God is a person who *remembers* his people. The revelation passage about the burning bush and Moses begins with the words:

God heard their groaning, and God *remembered* his covenant with Abraham, with Isaac, and with Jacob. And God saw the people of Israel, and he knew their condition (Ex 2:24–25).

God's memory is so indelible that it is stronger than that of a mother for her child:

> Can a woman forget her sucking child, that she should
> have no compassion on the son of her womb? Even
> these may forget, yet I will not forget you. Behold I have
> graven you on the palm of my hand so your walls are con-
> tinually before me (Is 49:15).

We note once again God's connection with the womb and
the maternal quality of child-remembrance. Once again like
God, the ideal Israelite *remembers* also. This was expressed
by the most precious text in the Bible for every Jew, called
the *Shemah Israel* from the opening words of the text,
"Hear, O Israel":

> Hear, O Israel: The Lord our God is one Lord; and you
> shall love the Lord your God with all your heart, and
> with all your soul, and with all your might. And these
> words which I command you this day shall be upon your
> heart; and you shall teach them diligently to your chil-
> dren, and shall talk of them when you sit in your house,
> and when you lie down, and when you rise. And you
> shall bind them as a sign upon your hand, and they shall
> be as frontlets between your eyes. And you shall write
> them on the doorposts of your house and on your gates
> (Deut 6:4–9).

We note the connection between heart and memory in
this text: "These words shall be upon your *heart.*" For the
Hebrews, the heart was the storehouse of memory. The wisdom teacher in Proverbs tells his "son" to write his words on
the tablet of his heart (3:3). In the New Testament Luke describes Mary as one who keeps the deeds of the infant Jesus
in her heart (1:59). In the *Shemah* text above, the image of
the Lord as the one loving God of his people is always to be
treasured in the heart. It was to be taught to children, the

subject of conversation at home, while traveling and at work. It was to be especially remembered when rising in the morning and when retiring at night. The words were to be as strongly engraved on memory as a tattoo on the hand or a mark between the eyes. They should be as evident as a sign on the house door or the gates of the house. Later Judaism applied the above words in a literal fashion. They were inscribed in parchment in small leather pouches that were placed over the heart, between the eyes, and wrapped about the wrists during times of prayer.

It would be hard to overestimate the power and influence of this text recited millions of times in the course of Jewish life and history. It was their central confession of faith. In obedience to the text, everyone recited the words morning and evening, at the synagogue, and often during the day. Jesus himself used them and pointed to them as part of a summary of the entire Torah (Mk 11:28–34; Mt 22:34–40; Lk 10:25–28). They were the first words that a father taught his child to speak. They were the last words that every Jew hoped to have on his/her lips.

The ideal of the *Shemah* as one's last words was modeled on Rabbi Akiba[12] in the second century A.D., who was tortured by the Romans and died for his faith. When the evening hour for reciting the Shemah arrived, he began to smile with joy. The Roman officer in charge asked him why he did so. The rabbi replied that all his life he had wanted to "love God with all his soul (life)" and now he had the opportunity to say these words of the *Shemah* with their fullest meaning as he died with them on his lips. Since Rabbi Akiba's time, millions of Jews have died with the *Shemah* as their last words. This was especially true in the Middle Ages and above all in history's darkest hour when German Nazis put millions of Jews to death in the infamous ovens of their death camps. Consequently, the words have a holiness and power hard to equal in human language since the whole life of so many millions of people was behind them even to the moment of their death.

In view of the importance of the *Shemah*, further attention to the text should be given: "Hear, O Israel. . . . You shall love the Lord your God with all your heart and with all your soul and with all your might." The word "love" is very action oriented, meaning to act out of love. In a very practical manner, this meant obedience to God and his commandments as the introductory words in Deuteronomy 6:1–3 indicate. The words "*Hear,* O Israel" signify obedience, surrender and openness to God in all of life. In fact, the root of the English word "obedience" comes from the Latin *obaudire,* meaning to hear or obey. Everything, including love and service of other people, was looked upon as obedience and personal service to God himself. It was a manifestation of his great love for all human beings.

The Jewish midrash on the *Shemah* is a valuable witness of tradition and practice in regard to this central confession of faith. Although actually put in written form around the sixth century, some of the rabbis quoted in the midrash go back to the second century, and may reflect even earlier tradition about its meaning. The midrash on the first verses above explain, "Love the Lord your God: that is, make him beloved among all creatures as did Abram." In other words, love for other people is a manifestation of God's own love and a direct service of him. This is reflected by Deuteronomy 10:12 which repeats the injunction to love and serve God with all the heart and soul, keeping the commandments. This is explained as being like God himself in his love for all people, especially the oppressed:

He executes justice for the fatherless and the widow, and loves the sojourner, giving him food and clothing.

> Love the sojourner, therefore; for you were sojourners
> in the land of Egypt (Deut 10:18–19).

This means there is a unity in all of life, with the one love of God prompting obedience to his commandments, especially those concerned with service of the needy.

The rabbinic midrash commentary brings out the complete dedication in the words, "with all your heart": "Let not your heart be divided—i.e., not wholly one—as regards your love for God." The combination "heart and soul" is often found together in the Bible as a reaffirmation of this totality. Behind the translation "soul" is the Hebrew *nephesh,* meaning a living being. Consequently, the midrash brings out that all of life must be behind this love, even if it means risking one's life. So the commentary reads, "Even if he takes your soul (i.e., your life). So it says, 'For thy sake we are slain every day' (Ps 44:22). Rabbi Simeon ben Azzai said, 'With all your soul,' that is, love him to the pressing out of the last drop of your life."

The words "with all your might" were interpreted by the midrash in reference to all of a person's substance or riches. Serving God with love must have priority over all earthly possessions and wealth. Later we will see in the New Testament that Matthew's Gospel seems influenced by the interpretation of the *Shemah* in ancient Jewish tradition.

The end product of the Deuteronomy text was not a subservient life, but complete vibrant living. The type of love envisioned there was considered a gift of God who alone could make it possible. It was imaged as an inner circumcision of the heart by God himself so life could be lived in this manner:

> And the Lord your God will circumcise your heart and
> the heart of your offspring, so that you will love the Lord

your God with all your heart and with all your soul, *that you may live* (Deut 30:6).

It was also an inner repentance or turning to God: "To return to the Lord your God, you and all your children, and obey his voice in all that I command you this day, with all your heart and with all your soul" (Deut 30:2). It was an inner relationship or cleaving to God in covenant: "To love the Lord your God and to walk in all his ways and to keep his commandments, and to *cleave* to him, and to serve him with all your heart and with all your soul" (Jos 22:5).

Summary

The *Shemah* represents the highest point of Jewish piety. Rabbinic commentary brought out the triple emphasis on heart-intensity, soul—the risk of life—and might—all of possessions and property. It was a formula of complete dedication and intensity that took in all of life-obedience to God and loving service of others. The repetition of this text daily and in important moments of life, even before death, gave the words unusual power and energy accompanied by the heart image. Countless Jewish martyrs especially in Hitler's Germany sealed the text with their own blood. Jesus used it as part of a summary of the whole Torah.

Exercise and Practice

There are few mantras in any language with as much energy and powerful imagery as the *Shemah*. Like Jesus, and so many millions of his fellow Jews, memorize it, especially the words, "You shall love the Lord your God with your whole heart and with your whole soul and with your whole strength." Use it as a precious mantra and repeat it morning and evening as well as during the day. To help by way of gesture and imagery, place your hand over your heart as you say, "With all your heart."

5
Jeremiah the Passionate Prophet
and the New Heart Covenant

Of all the prophets of Israel, Jeremiah is the one about whom we know most as a real human being. His book is most interesting to us because of the unusual prominence of heart language. He refers to the heart over sixty times. Heart language is used not only to express his own feelings toward God and toward his people, but also to describe God's feelings toward Israel and the type of conversion that God requires. Jeremiah has had lasting influence not only as messenger of hope for his people, but as a model to be taken up in the New Testament.

An outline of his life and times will help us better appreciate the significance of heart language in his prophecies. Jeremiah was born from a priestly family around 650 B.C. in the town of Anatoth near Jerusalem. While only a young man he was called to be a prophet. Because of his youth and lack of self-confidence, he was very reluctant to assume this role. However, he finally accepted after God assured him of his special protection (Jer 1:1–19). As a young man, his preaching seems to have been received with enthusiasm. This was due to the support of King Josiah. Under his reign a long-hidden or lost book of the law was found during repairs to the temple in the year 621 B.C. Part of this book is incorporated into Deuteronomy and the new spirit of total devotion to God that we described in the last chapter.

However, after the death of Josiah, Jeremiah became less and less popular. This was due to the strong stand that he took in regard to the new political situation. Babylon had been gradually extending its power over the whole Middle East. The Babylonian king offered Israel the possibility of becoming a vassal and thus becoming immune from attack and punishment. However, the Israelite king persisted in attempting to join military alliances with Egypt and other countries to resist the power of Babylon. The king also trusted that God would automatically take up the cause of his people and give them a victory over Babylon.

God told Jeremiah to tell his people and the nation's leaders that such a military solution was not according to the divine covenant with his people. There were no automatic guarantees that God would fight for Israel no matter what they did. Instead, they were to concentrate on the covenant God had made with them. The core of this agreement concerned justice for the poor and oppressed. In contrast, false prophets proclaimed that the temple itself was a sign of God's presence and protection for his people. Consequently, they could count on God's help against the Babylonians. In a typical encounter with such false prophets, Jeremiah stated:

> Do not trust in these deceptive words: "This is the temple of the Lord, the temple of the Lord, the temple of the Lord." For only if you truly amend your ways and your doings, if you truly execute justice one with another, if you do not oppress the alien, the fatherless or the widow, or shed innocent blood in this place . . . then I will let you dwell in this place, in the land that I gave of old to your fathers for ever (7:4–7).

The words of Jeremiah were a revolutionary threat to the military and government establishment. Jeremiah stood by his message and even told soldiers and people not to fight against the Babylonians. As a result, he was regarded as a traitor to his country. He was imprisoned and narrowly escaped death when thrown into a cistern to die (Jer 38). Even his home town rejected him and plotted to destroy him (11:18–23). On one occasion, he was bound in stocks and exposed to public ridicule (20:1–6).

As a result, Jeremiah felt very much alone. He was tempted at times to abandon his very difficult prophetic mission, a vocation that brought little response from people and untold suffering to himself. He did not have the usual support of wife and family. This was because God had told him, in view of the coming disaster at Babylon's hands, not to get married or to have children:

> This message came to me from the Lord: Do not marry any woman; you shall not have sons or daughters in this place, for thus says the Lord concerning the sons and daughters who will be born in this place . . . of deadly disease they shall die . . . (16:1–4).

In view of the extraordinary political and personal situation of Jeremiah, his use of heart language in regard to himself, his people, and even in regard to God has striking significance.

Personal Feelings

Jeremiah was no hard-nosed prophet impervious to the feelings of his people. He knew that his message was difficult, and he was deeply moved by the suffering people would bring on themselves by refusing to listen to it. Concerning false prophets, he says, "My heart is broken within me, all my bones shake" (23:9). He knows well the horrors of war that will come to Israel from following military leaders, and he feels this so deeply within himself that his heart knocks:

> My anguish, my anguish! I writhe in pain! Oh, the walls of my heart! My heart is beating wildly; I cannot keep silent; for I hear the sound of the trumpet, the alarm of war. Disaster follows hard on disaster, the whole land is laid waste (4:19–20).

His *heart* is filled with grief and he is sick over the whole matter (8:18). However, Jeremiah's feelings are not only identified with his own people, but even with those of their worst traditional enemies, the Moabites. His heart "wails like a flute" and moans because of their suffering (48:31).

In reference to God, Jeremiah's feelings were equally strong. He was tempted not to mention God any longer because of all the anguish that would come to him and his people: "The word of God has become for me a reproach and derision all day long" (20:8–9). However, God's word was like burning fire shut up in his heart that he could not hold in (20:9). He is confident that despite all the external adverse circumstances, God knows his heart (12:3). God's words mean so much to him that he "eats" them. Consequently he says, "Your words became to me a joy and the delight of my heart" (15:16).

Description of Unresponsive People

God really knows where the hearts of people are: "I the Lord search the heart" (17:10). The shocking image used is

that their state of the heart is worse than the physical un-
circumcision of pagans: all these nations are uncircumcised,
and all the house of Israel is uncircumcised in heart (9:26).
The sin of Judah is deeply rooted. It is engraved on the heart
(17:1). The total direction of their lives is toward gain and
violence: "You have eyes and heart only for your dishonest
gain, and for shedding innocent blood, and for practicing op-
pression and violence" (22:17). The people have been led as-
tray by false teachers and prophets: "How long shall there be
lies in the heart of the prophets who prophesy lies, and who
prophesy the deceit of their own heart" (23:26). This results
in deceit of the heart of the people (14:14; 49:16). Even despite the desolation of the land, a reminder to repent, no one
"lays it to heart" (12:11).

The Call to Change and Repentance

The language of Jeremiah reminds us of the reform language of Deuteronomy, especially the *Shemah*. Nothing less
than a complete turning to God and total dedication to him
will be enough. The direction of the heart must be completely changed. Jeremiah uses the "whole heart" terminol-
ogy of Deuteronomy: God complains that the people of
Judah have not returned with their whole heart, but in pretense (3:10). Yet he has confidence they will in the future
seek him with all their heart (29:13). Once again, the vivid
language of removing the outer covering of foreskin of the
heart is used: "Circumcise yourselves to the Lord, remove
the foreskin of your hearts" (4:4). As if it were a bundle of
dirty clothes, the heart needs to be washed clean: "O Jerusalem, wash your heart from wickedness that you may be
saved. How long shall your evil thoughts lodge within you?"
(4:14).

God Has a Heart

The God of Jeremiah is not a God of philosophical abstractions. He is a feeling, sensitive God deeply concerned for his people. The same heart language used of human beings is applied to God also. God turns to his people with the same intensity and devotion that he has asked of them: "I will rejoice in doing them good and I will plant them in this land in faithfulness, with all my heart and all my soul" (32:41). God will give them new leaders and shepherds who will faithfully mirror his own care for his people: "I will give you shepherds after my own heart who will feed you with knowledge and understanding" (3:15). In fact, it is probable that much of the anguish of Jeremiah himself is really the divine anguish of which the prophet is merely the mouthpiece.

In regard to God's heart language, Jeremiah stands out in the Bible for his use of the root *rachum,* womb-compassion, in regard to God. Despite Israel's sin and her resulting exile in Babylon, God announces that he will pluck his people up and bring them back home. Then he says, "After I have plucked them up, I will again have *compassion* on them, and I will bring them again each to his heritage and each to his land" (13:15). God will never reject his people, no matter what they have done. To the contrary, he says, "I will restore their fortunes, and will have *mercy* upon them. The use of *rachum* is all the more moving in a text describing God in terms of such womb-compassion for a child:

> Is Ephraim my dear son? Is he my darling child? For as
> often as I speak against him, I do remember him still.
> Therefore my *heart* yearns for him; I will surely *have*
> *mercy* on him. (31:20)

In fact, God's *rachum* is so irresistible that it will even cause the pagan king of Babylon to have the same *rachum* on Israel: "I will grant you mercy, that he may have mercy on you and let you remain in your own land" (42:12).

The New Heart Covenant as Hope for the Future

Why have so many people read and reread Jeremiah through the centuries? In exile and suffering, his message has given unshakable hope. Human beings often despair in face of their own weakness and repeated failures. They do not see a way they can really change. Jeremiah's message shows that the impossible can come about because it will be God who will make it happen: he will give the gift of a new heart to make it come about. Human weakness is reversed.

> I will give them a heart to know that I am the Lord: and they shall be my people and I will be their God, for they shall return to me with their whole heart (24:7).

Even though they may be scattered over all the world and divided, God will join them together once more:

> I will bring them back to this place, and I will make them dwell in safety. And they shall be my people, and I will be their God. I will give them one heart and one way, that they may fear me for ever, for their own good and the good of their children after them. I will make with them an everlasting covenant, that I will not turn away from doing to them: and I will put the fear of me in their hearts, that they may not turn from me. I will rejoice in doing them good, and I will plant them in this land in

faithfulness, with all my heart and all my soul (32:37–
41).

We note the unconditional nature of this covenant, so different from human covenants which are conditional, depending
on the other party's response. God will never change toward
his people and will even enable them to do their part as well.

The most remembered and influential message of God
through Jeremiah is the following promise of a new inner
covenant of the heart:

> Behold the days are coming, says the Lord, when I will
> make a new covenant with the house of Irael and the
> house of Judah, not like the covenant which I made with
> their fathers when I took them by the hand to bring them
> out of the land of Egypt, my covenant which they broke,
> though I was their husband, says the Lord (31:31–32).

The above text brings out a striking contrast. The old
covenant with Moses was an external law which was broken
by the people despite God's spousal love for them. A new
covenant will be given in the following terms:

> But this is the covenant which I will make with the house
> of Israel after those days, says the Lord: I will put my
> law within them, and I will write it upon their hearts;
> and I will be their God, and they shall be my people.
> And no longer shall each person teach their neighbors or
> brothers and sisters, saying, "Know the Lord," for they
> shall all know me from the least of them to the greatest,
> says the Lord; for I will forgive their iniquity, and I will
> remember their sin no more (31:33–34).

The unusual words above explain the true meaning of
the future heart covenant. Instead of the external words writ-

ten on stone tablets, it will be engraved on the heart. Since people often forget, God will make sure it is remembered by writing it on their hearts. The external law required readers, intermediaries, teachers and interpreters. But now the very least, even a child, will be able to experience it. Thus everything is a complete gift of love from God. Finally, complete and lavish forgiveness of sin is promised. Transgressions will not only be forgiven but even forgotten by God.

Summary

Jeremiah's use of heart language both in regard to himself and to God had a profound influence on Jewish history. It brought out God's sensitivity for his people and his unconditional love for them despite countless past failures. It gave new hope because their future success would be based not on their strength and achievements but on God's special gift of a new covenant written on their hearts and a total forgiveness of all their past sins that made possible a complete new start.

Jeremiah's New Heart Covenant and the New Testament

The second half of the book will deal in detail with New Testament texts, but in view of the exercise at the end of the next chapter, we will examine some New Testament eucharistic allusions to Jeremiah's new heart covenant. In describing the cup of the Eucharist, Paul, quoting Jesus, calls it "the new covenant in my blood" (1 Cor 11:25), thus using an expression (new covenant) only found in Jeremiah. The same words are also used in the institution narrative (longer Greek version) found in Luke 22:20. Matthew adds the words "for forgiveness of sins" (26:28) found equivalently at the end of Jeremiah 31:34. These references indicate that the early Church was aware that their celebration of the Eucharist was that of the new inner heart covenant promised by God through Jeremiah.

Exercises and Practices

Some of Jeremiah's striking heart images can be fruitfully used in heart imagery during meditation. For example, heart washing: "Jerusalem, wash your heart from wickedness, that you may be saved" (4:14), along with "I will forgive their iniquity, and I will remember their sin no more" (31:34). What so often weighs us down is guilt, a sense of failure about the past, time wasted, etc. We often envy the computer where files can so easily be permanently erased and forgotten so a new start can be made.

Building on previous heart awareness exercises and using the same start through concentration on the breath and in-between breath periods, focus on the heart region. Imagine it burdened and heavy with "filth" of the past: failures, hurts given or received, wounds not healed, etc. Then repeat God's words, "Wash your heart . . . that you may be saved." Imagine the Holy Spirit as a stream of living water washing and purifying your heart so it becomes as fresh and new as the day you were born. Begin life anew with this confidence as if today were the first day and the best day of your life. Repeat the expression "Today is the best day of my life" until you really believe it.

Other heart images of Jeremiah can also be used in a similar manner: the circumcision of the heart, or the visualization of God giving a new heart or writing his covenant on our hearts. The *new heart* imagery will be taken up in detail in the next chapter on the prophet Ezekiel's heart transplant operation.

6
Ezekiel the Psychic Prophet and His Pneumatic Heart Transplant

Like Jeremiah, Ezekiel was a prophet of the exile. Unlike Jeremiah, most of his teaching took place actually in Babylon among the exiles rather than in Israel. Ezekiel was among the first group of exiles to reach Babylon, perhaps about 597, before the destruction of Jerusalem. When they first arrived in Babylon, their physical conditions were not harsh; Ezekiel lived in his own house (3:24). Indeed the prophet Jeremiah had counseled the people not to look for a quick return but to settle down, build houses, live in them, plant gardens, eat of their produce, marry and raise children (29:5). The Babylonian rulers were not harsh to them but allowed them the freedom to do these things.

However, the psychological shock of the exile was quite another matter. Their own "God almighty" had proved to be a "loser," not able to protect his own temple which was destroyed in 587 B.C. They were now with foreign gods on foreign soil. They were tempted to consider the God of Israel as a local and territorial God who was helpless in Babylon. The people felt abandoned and deserted. God's dwelling place had been within his temple in the Holy of Holies. His holy covenant and place of powerful presence had been within the sacred ark of the covenant which was now lost to them.

Just to enter the capital of Babylon was a severe religious and cultural shock for the exiles. Their little capital at Jerusalem had a small population and was limited in size to about ten acres. Their temple was a small building of about 2,700 square feet. Babylon had an area of about a thousand acres with a population of about 200,000 composed of priests, freemen, and slaves from all over the world. The first place of worship the exiles could see from a distance was the Etemenanki, "the house of the platform of heaven and earth." This was a huge ziggurrat three hundred feet high and one hundred yards in length and breadth. No wonder their poor Hebrew God lost out against such overwhelming odds!

The prophet Ezekiel was regarded as an eccentric, a laughing stock to Babylonians and the butt of frequent jokes even among his own people. He stayed mostly to himself at home. He was regarded as a dreamer and impractical visionary given over at times to strange symbolic actions. Even the stories of his visions in the Bible are so mysterious that later Jewish teachers warned readers about them and forbade the reading of certain texts until the age of thirty years.

Ezekiel pondered and prayed over the meaning of this sad crisis for himself and his people. Had God's presence really left his people so they were now abandoned and deserted in a foreign land? Would it not be best to come to terms with the Babylonians and their victorious gods? One day an answer came to the prophet in the form of a mysterious vision. He saw a chariot coming down from heaven propelled by four mysterious flying creatures. Over the heads of the four creatures was a crystal firmament on the top of which the living God was enthroned (1:1–28).

Suddenly the impact of all of this struck Ezekiel. God's presence was no longer only in far off Jerusalem, but here in exile with his people. It began to dawn on him that God's temple was in his people wherever they might be. At this time Ezekiel was given his prophetic call. In the vision, a mysterious hand stretched out to him with a scroll within it. He was told to eat the scroll and go to speak to the house of Israel. He ate the scroll, understanding that God's message was to become part of his existence for the benefit of the people (2:1–10).

Ezekiel's visions had an awesome effect on his life and on his prophecies. The powerful presence of God even in exile became the dominant reality of his own life and his preaching. The spirit/breath of God is so prominent in his book that he has earned the title of the "pneumatic prophet." We have already cited his extraordinary vision and prophecy of "the dry bones" (Ez 37) where God breathes his spirit into the valley of Israel's dead bones in exile and gives them new life. In his own life, Ezekiel refers some ten times in his book to the spirit either coming upon him, lifting him up or carrying him away. He had a profound vision that God's spirit and presence would enable the building of a mysterious future temple. Underneath the altar of the temple he saw a mysterious fountain that issued as an ever-growing stream and gave life to the dead sea region, making it a new garden of Eden and source of life to the world (47:1ff).

Like Jeremiah, Ezekiel was concerned about the future of God's covenant once written by God's own hand on tablets of stone and kept within the ark of the covenant. The people had broken the covenant, and the ark itself was lost. What hope remained for them? It was true that the spirit of God was now present among the exiles, but how would this change their continued failure to keep the covenant that had been the cause of the exile? As in the case of Jeremiah, God revealed to Ezekiel that the cause lay in the heart, and only God's gift of a new heart would enable the people to keep the covenant.

This brings us to some of the most dramatic and unusual texts in the Bible, Ezekiel's heart transplant visions in 11:19–20, 18:31 and especially 36:26–27. They are remarkable for their conjunction of spirit and heart in a very concrete ethical context. The mention of Spirit goes all the way through the Bible, but here for the first time in exile,[13] spirit is used in an ethical context as the transforming agent of the heart. God's prophecy through Ezekiel makes use of heart-transplant imagery to provide people with a most powerful means of meditation and conviction that God is able to transform their hearts so that they can keep his commandments in the form of real compassion and love for the oppressed. It is interesting to reflect that although the heart-transplant operation has become an actuality only in recent years, people have known about its imagery for thousands of years and used it effectively.

First it would be well to have the text before us so we can comment in detail. The text reads as follows:

> I will give you a new heart and I will place within you a new spirit. I will take away from your flesh the heart of stone, and I will give you a heart of flesh. I will put my spirit within you so you will walk in my commandments as well as keep and observe my statutes. You shall live in the land I gave to your fathers; you shall be my people and I will be your God (36:26–28).

First of all, to study the text, let us situate it within its context, which is that of 36:16–38. There, a great reversal of

God's action is promised after the people's previous conduct and their punishment in exile (36:16–20). Because the people have defiled God's name, he will intervene not for their sake but to honor his own name (36:21–23). He will bring them back to their land. However, because the land is holy, he will first cleanse and purify them from their impurities and abominations.

We can point out the following areas of meaning in the text:

1. God's work alone can renew his people. It is his supreme gift. Three times the word "give" or "put" is repeated in the text. This is from the *natan* root in Hebrew while the Greek has *dōsō*, "I will give or place."

2. In connection with #1, the spirit is the agent of change. It is called a "new spirit" or "my spirit." In reality, "new spirit" and "new heart" are not to be taken separately but together as in 18:31 where we have "new heart and new spirit." W. Eichrodt[14] notes that spirit and heart are not to be taken in an additional sense but as side by side since the spirit has the special function to bring the heart into conformity with the divine will.

3. The heart change or conversion is in the form of a "transplant." We have seen in the Bible that the heart is the special place of God's action to transform the will and human activity. The psalmist (51:12) echoes the view that only God can change the heart, so this must be requested through prayer: "Create for me a clean heart, O God, and renew within me a right spirit." Here spirit and heart go together as in Ezekiel. The prophet dramatizes this change by the image of the removal of an impervious heart of stone and the substitution of a heart of flesh in its place.

4. Radical ethical implications. The change occurs to sensitize the heart (a heart of flesh) so the people will listen

to God and obey his commandment (36:27). The heart is directly connected to such sensitive listening. We have seen that, in asking for wisdom, Solomon asked for literally a "listening heart" so he could judge his people (1 Kgs 3:9). The type of conversion envisioned is not that of keeping legal religious observances but of returning to the core of the covenant in the form of responsibilities to other people. Before the parallel text of 18:31 ("Get yourselves a new heart and a new spirit"), Ezekiel indicates that a heart of flesh means real sensitivity to the needs of others, especially the oppressed. Ezekiel states that the righteous person is one who "does not wrong anyone . . . but gives his bread to the hungry, and covers the naked with a garment" (18:16–17).

5. The inheritance of the land as true obedient sons. The end result of the text is to enable the people to really live once more in the land given to their *fathers*. This is an inheritance given by God and then passed on from father to son through the generations.

6. We note the difference between these words and God's words written on stone in the old lost ark of the covenant. The covenant is now a spirit-transformed heart as a special gift of God. The startling truth is revealed that this heart-transplant is the new holy ark of the covenant made possible by the spirit of God. The new sensitive heart of flesh makes genuine love and compassion of others a reality.

In our next chapter we will see some of the startling effects that Ezekiel's heart transplant text had on the apostle Paul and his teaching.

Summary

The exiles thought they had lost God's presence and help in a foreign country, where they were being punished for their sins. They were tempted to despair and felt a keen sense of helplessness as they remembered their past failures. God used Ezekiel as an unusual instrument to teach his people that his powerful spirit was still present among them. This spirit would effect an inner substitution of God's own heart of love and compassion so they would be able to keep his commandments and be worthy to return to their holy land.

Exercises and Practice

1. Ezekiel's heart transplant text is one of the most powerful images ever used for personal renewal. This type of approach is found not only in Ezekiel thousands of years ago, but in Patanjali, a Hindu mystic and teacher (around Jesus' time), who wrote about a practice that went back centuries before him: "Concentration may be obtained . . . by meditating on the heart of an illumined soul that is free from passion."[15] The following is a suggested way of using it, keeping in mind Jeremiah's heart covenant in the last chapter and its connection with the Eucharist.

Start off by repeating to yourself the text "I will give you a new heart and I will place within you a new spirit. I will take away from your flesh the heart of stone, and I will give you a heart of flesh." Do this until you have memorized it, and then keep repeating it with a deeper and deeper trust that God is able to do what he promises, and enable you to transform your life no matter how much failure there may have been in the past.

(Keep in mind that a relaxed state is necessary in order to use eidetic heart images, and conscious breathing is the best way to attain this.) Use the breathing exercises in Chapter 2 to help you. Gradually focus your breathing on various parts of the body and then concentrate it on the heart. Now imagine the heart of some great person that you admire.

Here, to avoid confusion, we will use the heart of Christ, but it could be the heart of Mary or some other saint or respected person of history.

Imagine Christ in a scene blessing and hugging little children. Then go to his heart and try to identify with the love that he feels toward them. (Spend as much time as you wish on each area to obtain its full fruit.) To comprehend the extent of this love, imagine the love of your mother toward you as shown in some incident(s). Then gradually move to the loving hearts of countless millions of mothers in the world—and even through history. Unite them all together in the heart of Christ, picturing it to expand to include them all. (At each step, try to absorb as much warmth and energy as possible.) Then go on to any or all of the following areas, using the same steps: e.g., the love of your father to you, all fathers, etc., uniting all this in the heart of Christ's love for children. Other possibilities could include the love of friends and spouses, thinking of Jesus' love for Mary Magdalene and the twelve, or the love of children for their parents, like that of Jesus for Mary and Joseph; or picture the compassion and care of a doctor or nurse, then Jesus' love for the sick, the mentally ill, etc., or Jesus' concern for the poor and oppressed, his love for his enemies, e.g., Judas, or for those who failed him (Peter). Finally put this all together in the heart of Christ, moving on to the incarnate Word as the great compassionate heart-beat of the universe. Absorb as much as you can from this powerful image.

Now recall again God's firm promise: "I will give you a new heart and place within you a new spirit." Imagine Jesus at the Last Supper, keeping this promise in mind and saying, "Take and eat; this is my body." Understand these words as inviting you to complete oneness with him, especially with his heart, the great heart-throb of the universe that you have just pictured. See your own heart of stone being melted and transformed into a spirit-transformed heart of flesh as promised by Ezekiel. Spend as much time as you can absorbing the energy and warmth of this image. Keeping in mind the ethical dimensions of Ezekiel, turn your heart and attention to someone who needs help and imagine some concrete expression of this that will take place in the very near future.

2. Keep the ethical dimensions of the heart-transplant text as a continual challenge before you. Ezekiel did not speak of only inner change, but of an outward expression that went with it. Jeremiah, Ezekiel and others were really revolutionaries of their time. They felt that religion had everything to do with politics, as well as economics and social realities. For Ezekiel, in the text quoted above, we saw that a transformed heart meant that all the hungry would have enough to eat, and that the poor would be adequately clothed, and that all people would receive justice. This is a basic political as well as religious statement. It would mean, for example, that the function of government is to assure that *all* have enough, rather than guaranteeing special benefits for any group. And of course, if the poor are to have enough, it means that all will have to receive less, given the limitations of the earth's resources. Yet Ezekiel would say that no political system of itself will ever succeed on its own, however just its principles may seem. The human heart tends to be "stony," and only God's gift can really transform it into a heart of flesh and compassion. Thus true religion, and a just economic and political system, can never stand on their own but must be effectively united. Both need each other.

7
The Secret of Paul the Apostle:
A Heart-Spirit Transformation

Western Christianity as we know it is largely due to the unbelievable activity of one man, Paul the apostle. What was the secret of his extraordinary success? There is little in his Jewish background that can account for it. He was as thorough a Jew as any contemporary, and even more so if we take literally what he writes to the Philippians:

> If any other man thinks he has reason for confidence in the flesh, I have more: circumcised on the eighth day, of the people of Israel, of the tribe of Benjamin, a Hebrew born of Hebrews: as to the law a Pharisee, as to zeal a persecutor of the church, as to righteousness under the law blameless (3:4–6).

Yet a radical change came over him that was completely unexpected. He describes it in this way:

> But whatever gain I had, I counted as loss for the sake of Christ. Indeed I count everything as loss because of the surpassing worth of knowing Christ Jesus my Lord. For his sake I have suffered the loss of all things, and count

them as refuse, in order that I may gain Christ and be found in him not having a righteousness of my own, based on law, but that which is through faith in Christ (3:7–9).

The above text indicates that his whole life took a new direction in the form of total living service of Christ. He writes to the Galatians that he felt so identified with Christ that there seemed to be a new independent power at work within him:

I have been crucified with Christ: it is no longer I who live, but Christ who lives in me; and the life I now live in the flesh I live by faith in the Son of God, who loved me and gave himself for me (2:20).

What brought about this dramatic change in his life? What was it that transformed him so completely? Everything starts with the impact of his conversion which was a heart/spirit experience that completely reversed the direction of his whole life. S. Kim's study[16] of the origins of Paul's Gospel has focused attention on 2 Corinthians 4:6 as a description of Paul's own experience.

For it is God who said "Let light shine out of darkness" who has shone in our hearts to give the light of the knowledge of God's glory in the face of Christ.

In his study, Kim first counters the objection that, rather than the Damascus conversion event, Paul is describing a typical Christian experience as in 2 Corinthians 3:18 where he writes that "all of us" are gazing on the Lord's glory with unveiled faces and being transformed from glory to glory. In response, Kim points out that the subject in 4:6

is Paul and his companions rather than the Christian community. This is because Paul distinguishes in the next verse (4:5) between "ourselves" and the Corinthians toward whom the apostles are servants. Also in the same verse Paul writes, "We do not preach ourselves." Preaching is the distinctive work of Paul and his companions, not the average Christian. So the context of 4:6 would point to Paul and his companions, especially Paul himself.

In addition, the text above accords well with other descriptions Paul makes of his conversion. The words, "God's glory on the face of Christ," point to a vision of the risen Christ as in 1 Corinthians 15:8 and 1 Corinthians 9:1. The reference to God shining in the heart is similar to the interior description of Galatians 1:16 where Paul writes that God "was pleased to reveal his Son in me." The 2 Corinthians 4:6 text also has a conversion "new beginnings" atmosphere to it. The old creation began when God said, "Let light shine out of darkness." Paul's "beginnings" are parallel and similar: God shines his light on Paul's heart so he can be a witness of the resurrection of Christ in the new age. This conversion experience seems to be in mind when Paul states that "if anyone is in Christ he is a new creation" (2 Cor 5:17). Thus the text reflects a "once and for all" experience that is a complete new beginning. This differs from the community picture of transformation in 3:18, where there is question of a progress "from one degree of glory to another."

The place of 2 Corinthians 4:6 as a conversion text is strengthened also by the secondary and later description of Paul's conversion found in the Acts of the Apostles. Corresponding to the shining light from God in 2 Corinthians, Paul's conversion in Acts begins with a "light from heaven" (9:3; 22:6). The wording of the conversion account in Acts 26:13 is also similar to 2 Corinthians 4:6. The former text has "a light shone around me," while the latter relates that God "has shone his light."

This brings us to the important conjunction of spirit and heart in Paul's conversion experience. First of all, in reference to the heart, Paul described his vision as God shining the light-glory of the risen Christ directly in his heart. In view of the Hebrew conviction that the heart is the center of God's action, this is Paul's way of saying that this has profoundly affected his entire being. This totality is reflected in Paul's insistence that faith must come from the heart:

> The word is near you, on your lips and in your heart . . .
> because if you confess with your lips that Jesus is Lord
> and believe in your heart that God raised him from the
> dead, you will be saved. For a person believes with the
> heart and so is justified, and he confesses with the lips
> and is so saved (Rom 10:8–10).

We note the triple reference to the heart in the above text. The same theme of the centrality of the heart is also found in Romans 5:5; 6:17; 2 Corinthians 1:22; 3:2–3; 3:15; Galatians 4:6.

Secondly, in reference to the Spirit, we do not find it directly mentioned in 2 Corinthians 4:6, but it is actually behind the whole experience. Paul elsewhere states that Jesus' resurrection in glory is directly caused by the Spirit: "The Spirit of him who raised Christ Jesus from the dead" (Rom 8:11). Also, a resurrection body of glory is only made possible by the action of the Spirit (1 Cor 15:42–47).

We may conclude then that there are important indications that the conversion experience of Paul was in terms of spirit and heart. This experience transformed his whole life as well as his teaching and theology. The effect of this heart/

spirit theme will be even more powerful if it can be shown that Paul was also influenced by the heart conversion and heart transplant texts we have seen in Jeremiah and Ezekiel, especially the latter.

The Prophetic Heart/Spirit
Ezekiel Text and Paul

The importance of heart and spirit in his conversion no doubt prompted Paul to reflect on the principal heart/spirit texts in the Hebrew Scriptures, especially those of Ezekiel in the last chapter. What is so unusual about Ezekiel is that he connects the spirit with concrete ethical renewal, something not directly found in other texts about the spirit. This spirit-connected ethical renewal would be extremely important for Paul in his preaching. This can be better brought out if we contrast Ezekiel's heart/spirit text with other principal Old Testament texts that speak of a future outpouring of the spirit.

First of all, Joel 2:28–29 describes the coming gift of the spirit in the last times with these words:

> And it shall come to pass afterward that I will pour out my spirit upon all flesh; your sons and daughters shall prophesy, your old men shall dream dreams, and your young men shall see visions: Even upon the men servants and the maid servants in those days I will pour out my spirit.

However Joel stresses psychic signs such as dreams and prophecy rather than ethical conversion.

The prophet Zechariah has this pronouncement, "I will pour out on the house of David and Jerusalem's inhabitants a spirit of compassion and supplication" (12:10). Here the context is more in terms of general repentance and prayer. Isaiah 11:2 describes the spirit resting on a future descendant of David, conferring on him the ethical qualities of wisdom, counsel, understanding, justice, etc. However, this spirit gift is for the messianic king, not all the people. In Isaiah 42:1–4, the spirit will come upon a chosen servant who will bring forth justice to the nation. This picture, however, is more in terms of a world mission rather than personal ethical renewal. Isaiah 44:3 declares, "I will pour out my spirit upon your descendants, and my blessing upon your offspring." This text contains few further details and seems to describe a future general blessing for all people. In Isaiah 61:1, the prophet announces that the Lord's spirit is upon him to announce a jubilee year of favor from God that will mean good news to the captives, to the lowly and prisoners. However, in this text the gift of the spirit seems tied to the prophet's impulse to proclaim this message.

In contrast, the Ezekiel text is very explicitly one of a heart transformation by the spirit in order to effect a great ethical renewal of all the people. In addition, it is the only prophetic text with the direct conjunction of spirit and heart. It is not uncommon to find commentaries with textual allusions to Ezekiel in the spirit/heart passages. However, a detailed examination of some key Pauline texts will show indications that the heart/spirit transplant of Ezekiel may be very much in Paul's teaching as he reflects on the meaning of his own heart/spirit conversion.

Galatians 4:6–7

Because you are sons, God has sent the Spirit of his Son into our hearts crying "Abba, Father," so that you are no longer a slave but a son, and if a son, an heir.

The verses preceding the above text suggest that Paul is referring to fulfillment of Old Testament Scriptures. He writes, "When the time had fully come, God sent his Son, born of a woman, born under the law to redeem those who were under the law that we might receive adoption as sons" (4:4–5). The idea of "fullness of time" seems to refer to Scripture fulfillment, for Paul uses the verb "fulfill" in terms of completing the requirements of the written Torah. In Galatians 5:14, he writes that the whole law is fulfilled in one saying. (Cf. also Rom. 13:8, 10; 8:4.)

If Paul is thinking of Old Testament fulfillment, there are four remarkable similarities to Ezekiel 36:25–28: the initiative of God, the work of the Spirit, the locus of the heart and the obedience of sonship. The first, God's initiative, is very evident in the words "God sent his Son" (v. 4) and "God has sent the Spirit of his Son" (v. 6). The second element of the Spirit is so dominant that the Spirit seems to be even working independently in crying out "Abba, Father." O. Betz[17] has argued that the Romans 8:16 parallel text even seems to be a corrective to Galatians in its statement that the Spirit gives testimony together with our spirit, rather than alone. The third area, the locus of the heart, is quite evident. It is here where the action of the Spirit takes place. As in the Ezekiel text, spirit and heart go together. In fact, the only Old Testament locus for their conjunction in an eschatological conjunction is Ezekiel. The transformation in Ezekiel is emphasized through the change from a heart of stone to a heart of flesh. The transformed heart in Galatians is that of a person who was a slave but now a son. We will see that heart and Spirit will also go together in Romans 5:5 and 2 Corinthians 1:1–3. To emphasize the change, Ezekiel has both the words "new spirit" and "my spirit."

The final common element in Galatians and Ezekiel is

that of obedience. While Galatians does not use the actual word, that meaning is very evident. The contrast in Galatians is not from slavery to total freedom but to the status of son. In the common heredity customs of the time, the son ultimately became a co-owner, but subject in obedience to his father. The words "Abba, Father" are to be understood as a cry of obedience. In discussing the parallel text of Romans 8:15, Kasemann[18] notes that they should be understood in terms of "radical obedience."

However, Paul makes some distinct changes from the sense of Ezekiel. First of all there is the mediatorship of Christ that makes the transformation possible. God sends his Son (4:4) or the Son's Spirit (4:6) to make this come about. In this connection, Paul has thoroughly personalized Ezekiel's message. A person becomes God's child not by obedience alone but by union and identification with Jesus. This identification is so strong that Paul writes in Galatians that God's commandments and law are summed up in one word, "You shall love your neighbor as yourself" (5:14). Later Paul will call this "the law of Christ" (6:2).

Romans 5:5

Hope does not disappoint us because love of God is poured in our hearts through the Holy Spirit which has been given to us.

In this text we have five elements common to Ezekiel's heart transplant: the gift, the Spirit, the heart, obedience, and the ethical goal. The "Holy Spirit which has been given to us" emphasizes complete initiative and gift. It corresponds to the triple giving we have seen in Ezekiel. The gift is that of the Spirit which has the same transformative force as in Ezekiel. It changes the *heart* so it becomes the bearer and instrument of the love of God which is the ethical element.

This "love of God," *agapē tou theou,* could have either the sense of an objective "love for God" or a subjective "love of God" if we looked only at this verse. However, since Paul proceeds to explain its meaning in the next verses, it can only be taken in a subjective sense as referring to a share in God's love for human beings. In the next verse, Paul writes that Christ died for the wicked at the designated time. Then he states that God showed his love for us by this death (v. 8). This indicates that "love of God" means specifically God's great unconditional love for mankind as manifested in the death of Christ.

The final element of obedience is also here implicitly. In Philippians, Paul explains that the essential element in Christ's loving death was that he became "obedient unto death" (2:8). In Romans, Paul concludes that one man's obedience has brought all to justice (5:19). Thus we see that obedient sonship (as in Ezekiel) is behind the Romans text and the source of the ethical sense in God's love. This love in the believer goes far beyond laws and precepts, so Paul will note in Romans 13:8 that "he who loves his neighbor has fulfilled the law," and also in 13:10, "Love is the fulfillment of the law."

We can conclude that several indications point to at least the imagery in Ezekiel as Paul writes Romans 5:5. Paul's unique emphasis is the stress on the Spirit instilling the love of God into a transformed human heart that loves others with the same love as that of God and Christ. The Son's obedience in Galatians becomes in Romans a total love for others.

2 Corinthians 3:3–4

You show that you are a letter of Christ delivered by us, a letter written not with ink but with the Spirit of the living God, not on tablets of stone but on tablets of flesh in hearts.

The text has the Spirit, heart, flesh, and covenant elements as in Ezekiel. The expression for "flesh in hearts" is verbally the same as the Greek Old Testament text for Ezekiel 36:26, "hearts of flesh." The expression "written on your hearts" appears influenced by Jeremiah's heart covenant in 31:33, "I will write it (my law) on your hearts." The covenant theme is found a few verses later in Paul where he states that he has become a minister of a *new covenant*, in contrast to the old (3:14). We have also the explicit mention of new covenant in Jeremiah's heart covenant text of 31:31. Once again Paul has introduced a new element as he reflects on the heart texts of Ezekiel and Jeremiah. It is Christ who writes a letter in the heart with the Spirit of the living God. Paul only delivers it as a faithful minister.

There are other texts in Paul that may be influenced by Ezekiel, but not as directly as those above. Paul in 2 Corinthians 1:21–22 refers to God who has "given us his Spirit in our hearts as a guarantee." Here we have together the element of gift, as in the triple giving of Ezekiel, the Spirit and the heart. Other texts only mention the gift or promise of the Spirit as in 2 Corinthians, 5:5, 1 Thessalonians 4:8, Romans 8:16, and Galatians 3:14.

Conclusion

Paul wrote in 2 Corinthians 4:6 that God has shone in hearts to reveal the glory of God shining on the face of

Christ. There are indications that this text describes Paul's own conversion experience, one in which the images of spirit and heart are central. This appears to have led Paul to emphasize the great eschatological texts of a spirit-effected heart transplant in Ezekiel 36:26–28 and the heart covenant in Jeremiah, especially 31:33–34. However, Paul has transformed these texts by making the Spirit (through Christ) the mediator of a new covenant based on love. The wording of the Supper of the Lord also suggests that Paul thought of the Eucharist in terms of a new heart covenant (cf. the chapter on Jeremiah).

Exercise and Application

Paul's conversion was not from a bad to a good life but from a life dominated by Torah and duty to a new passionate Christo-centric life. Formerly, he was trying to do all he was supposed to do, but somehow it was not enough. In some respects, we can identify with him in our own lives. Most of us try hard to fulfill our duties to family, profession, country, one another and ourselves—which of course is praiseworthy. But at some time or other, our energy lags and we tire out. We often feel that there is no passionate direction of our lives. This is a sign that new priorities need to be made. The following is a suggested way to participate in Paul's conversion experience through heart and spirit images. Paul himself suggested that our experience could be similar to his when he wrote:

> And we all, with unveiled face beholding the glory of the Lord, are being changed into his likeness from one degree of glory to another; for this comes from the Lord who is the Spirit (2 Cor 3:18).

The Greek word used in the text for "change into his likeness" is from the root *metamorphosis,* translated into Latin as *transfiguratio.* It is the same word used in the Gospel story of Jesus' transfiguration (e.g. Matthew 17:1–8) about which Paul is perhaps thinking. Consequently, we can use the transfiguration story as a background for our meditation exercise that follows:

After some relaxing breathing time, close your eyes and imagine that Jesus has invited you also to climb a high mountain with Peter, James and John in the Gospel story. Picture the difficult climb as you also reflect on your own difficult "climbs" as you strive to fulfill the duties and responsibilities of each day. When you reach the mountain top, the sun is near the horizon. Jesus is praying with his back to the sun. You notice that the sun rays go through his body transfiguring it with light, while his face becomes radiant and glowing.

In your imagination, you draw near to him, opening your heart to experience this wonderful energy. As you do this, some burning light rays from Jesus come into your heart and body, filling them with light, warmth and energy. Stop to feel and experience this as deeply as possible. Looking around you, you notice that Peter, James and John are also radiant with the light of Jesus' transfiguration. Suddenly a cloud passes over you. Afterward, all of them look the same as they were when you climbed the mountain together. Jesus reminds you that you can experience this energizing transfiguration any time that faith and prayer prompt your eyes and heart to do so.

As you come down from the mountain filled with radiant joy and energy, you begin to reflect on the various areas of your life. You examine them in the light of the personal *metamorphosis* you have experienced that makes you identified with Christ's indescribable love and energy. How will this affect, for example, your friends, your relationships, your profession, your political activity, your local community and Church activity, your leisure time, etc.?

Paul's great secret of success was this *metamorphosis* and identification with Christ.[19] It is a secret that can be shared by every sincere believer.

8
Matthew's Heart Catharsis

Matthew's great concern is to show that Jesus has taught the highest ideal of perfection and love possible to a human being. This means imitation of God himself as described in Jesus' words:

> So that you may be sons of your Father who is in heaven;
> for he makes his sun rise on the evil and on the good,
> and he sends rain on the just and the unjust (5:45).

In the Sermon on the Mount, Matthew presents a summary of Jesus' teaching to show that it fulfills and even goes beyond the highest perfection previously presented in traditional teachings. Jesus states, "Think not that I have come to abolish the law and the prophets; I have come not to abolish them but to fulfill them. . . . Unless your righteousness exceeds that of the scribes and Pharisees, you will never enter the kingdom of heaven" (5:17–20).

In Chapter 4 we saw that the Jewish *Shemah* summed up the Jewish ideal with its injunction of total love of God—"with all your heart and soul," according to Deuteronomy 6:4. Matthew likewise is concerned to present the *Shemah* in its highest form. During Jesus' final teaching in

Jerusalem, a scribe tested him with the question, "Teacher, which is the greatest commandment in the law?" (22:36). Jesus replied,

> You shall love the Lord your God with all your heart, and with all your soul, and with all your mind. This is the greatest and the first commandment. And a second is like it: You shall love your neighbor as yourself. On these two commandments depend all the law and the prophets (22:37–40).

"The greatest and the first commandment" could have no equal for Jesus or for the Jews because it spoke of a complete and total love for God. How then could the second be "like it"? A surprising answer comes from looking at the context of "You shall love your neighbor as yourself," found in Leviticus 19:18. The section begins with the words, "You shall not hate your brother in your *heart*" (19:17). In the texts, neighbor, sons of your own people and brother are all in parallel. What likeness then is there to the first commandment to love God? Both the command to love God and the command in reference to one's brother contain the same word "heart." A total love of God must necessarily include loving one's neighbor from the heart also. In contrast, a heart with hatred toward a brother or neighbor could not possibly be the "with all your heart" complete love of God. This above interpretation of the full meaning of the *Shemah* will form a central theme in Matthew's Gospel.

Gerhardsson's book, *The Ethos of the Bible*,[20] presents the whole Gospel of Matthew as built around Jewish interpretation of the *Shemah*. In Chapter 4 we presented the midrash on Deuteronomy 6:4–6 with its triple heart, soul and strength injunction to love/serve God. The rabbinic commentators explained that "all of the heart" referred to one's inner and outer desires and longings; "the whole soul" meant that we must be ready to face even death in our readiness to obey God's commands. "The whole strength" meant that the entirety of one's resources (property, wealth, power, status) should be behind our resolve.

Gerhardsson tried to show that all of Matthew's Gospel is built around this triple early explanation of the *Shemah.* While some of Gerhardsson's applications may be a little far-fetched, his treatment of the parable of the sower and the temptations of Jesus are particularly impressive. We will try to summarize his interpretation as follows:

First of all Matthew introduces the explanation of the parable by a double reference to the heart from Isaiah to explain why people do not understand Jesus' parables. It is a question of where their hearts are:

> This people's heart has grown dull, and their ears are heavy of hearing and their eyes they have closed, lest they should perceive with their eyes and hear with their ears, and understand with their heart, and turn for me to heal them (6:9–10).

Then, following the outlines of rabbinic exegesis on the *Shemah,* Gerhardsson notes that the parable of the sower focuses on three types of hearers who do not receive the word about the kingdom in an enduring way. The farmer sows the seed which falls on the pathway, on rocky soil, among thorns, and finally on good earth (13:4–23). In the first case, on the pathway, the hearers have no depth of understanding and the devil snatches what was sown *in the heart.* These people have no real desire to know. They are those who do not conform to the first part of the *Shemah* "with all your heart" referring to the inner desires.

The second group is represented by the rocky soil. They receive the word joyfully as long as there is no crisis or trouble, but when persecution or suffering comes, they quickly wither up and die because they have no deep roots. This conforms to the second part of the *Shemah* "with your whole soul (or life)." They are literally afraid for their lives, and are not willing to risk them in any way.

The third group does indeed hear the word, but earthly cares and concern for riches divide their attention so that these "weeds and thorns" choke and kill the word. These people correspond to the third group of the *Shemah* who do not love God "with all their strength," which means external possessions, riches, prestige, etc.

The fourth group is represented by the seeds that fall on good receptive earth. They understand the word and bear a really "impossible" hundredfold harvest. In contrast to the first group which lacks understanding in their hearts, these comprehend from this deep inner source. Matthew does not repeat the word "heart" for this fourth group, but he presupposes it. Luke is more explicit in completing the contrast by referring to them as people who hold fast to the word with an honest and good *heart* (8:15).

The sower parable is really Jesus' life-style in story form as a model for imitation. Matthew's Gospel emphasizes discipleship. Disciples are asked to follow or imitate Jesus some twenty-four times in Matthew, more than in any other Gospel. The introductory temptation of Jesus presents him as a model to follow based on the total dedication presented in the *Shemah* as explained in rabbinic interpretation brought out by Gerhardsson.

"He fasted forty days and forty nights, and afterward he was hungry" (4:2). The first temptation involves acute hunger: "The tempter came and said to him, 'If you are the Son of God, command these stones to become loaves of bread.' " According to the *Shemah* midrash, the desires dividing the heart, especially food, drink, sex, etc., often conflict with total dedication of the heart to God. Satan tempts Jesus to satisfy his hunger through a miracle just as Israel did in the wilderness. Jesus replies in the words of Scripture that his true bread is the word of God: "A person does not live by bread alone but by every word that proceeds from the mouth of God" (4:4). In other words, Jesus must be obedient to God who does not wish him to provide for himself by acts of power. Thus the first temptation corresponds to the first part of the *Shemah,* "with all your heart," instead of with a divided heart.

In the second temptation, the devil asks Jesus to throw himself down from the temple pinnacle, and thus force God to intervene miraculously to save him. Jesus again replies through Scripture that God is not to be tempted, in this case by demanding that God save him from death. Thus Jesus conforms to the second part of the *Shemah* "with all your soul (life)."

In the third temptation Satan brings Jesus to a high mountain and shows him all the kingdoms of the world with their splendor and glory. The devil promises all these to Jesus if he will worship him and follow his plans. This third temptation corresponds to the third part of the *Hear, O Israel* with its phrase "with all your strength," interpreted by the rabbis as referring to all of one's riches, power, prestige and possessions.

The three great temptations of Christ are those faced by Jesus' disciples throughout the Gospel. The beginning of Jesus' ministry is paralleled by the end when Jesus is tempted on the cross before his death. The wording is similar to Satan's three temptations after Jesus' baptism, with their references to Son of God, the temple, the king of Israel and saving himself by miraculously coming down from the cross.

Matthew's Heart Catharsis

We have seen that Matthew has made the heart a symbol of total dedication. I wish to suggest that the theme of heart catharsis is also in his mind as he presents Jesus' teachings. The first indications of this appear in the Sermon on the Mount (Mt 5–7). Jesus announces in the introductory beatitudes, "Blessed are the clean of heart" (*hoi katharoi tē kardia*) (5:8). This cleanness of heart is a familiar motif from the psalms, especially 51:12 where the writer prays, "Create in me a clean heart, O God" (cf. also 73:1; 24:4). It is also similar to the heart/spirit text in Ezekiel 36:25–28 which begins with the phrase, "I will purify you" (*kathariō*). Heart cleansing is essential because the heart is the central place where the will acts. If the heart is clogged or filled with uncleanness, a person's actions and words will likewise be unclean. If it is filled with the Spirit and love, every word and action will be moved by love and kindness.

Jesus announces this double possibility of the heart in Matthew 12:34–35 as follows:

> The mouth speaks from the abundance of the heart. The good person from his good treasure brings out good things. The evil person from his evil treasure brings out evil.

Jesus also makes a dramatic contrast between eating "unclean foods" which cannot defile a person because they are from the outside and speaking from an unclean heart which defiles everything a person does:

> Do you not see that whatever goes *into* the mouth passes into the stomach and so passes on? But what *comes out of* the mouth proceeds from the *heart,* and this defiles a person. For out of the *heart* come evil thoughts, murder, adultery, fornication, theft, false witness, slander. These are what defile a person: but to eat with unwashed hands does not defile anyone (15:17–20).

Going back to the Sermon on the Mount, we can see how this heart catharsis influences Jesus' teaching. Jesus emphasizes that real observance of the ten commandments must be accompanied by an interior disposition of the heart. For example,

> You have heard that it was said of old, "You shall not kill; and whoever kills shall be liable to judgment." But I say to you that everyone who is angry with his brother shall be liable to judgment (5:21–22).

In the Bible, the heart is the place where anger and hatred reside. So the text of Leviticus 19:17 states, "You shall not hate your brother in your heart." We have already seen that Matthew associates this text with the interpretation of the *Shemah.* The commandment not to murder a brother or sister means that there is responsibility also for an inner "murder" that takes place in the heart.

The same spirit applies to the commandment, "You shall not commit adultery." Jesus comments, "I say to you that everyone who looks at a woman lustfully has already committed adultery with her in his *heart*" (5:28). It should be noted that here and elsewhere some modern translations, such as the New American Bible, use "thoughts" or "mind" as a translation for the literal Greek word "heart." However, this type of translation weakens the full emotional impact of Jesus' teaching.

How can a radical heart cleansing take place in the above situations and others? Matthew does not present a complete program of heart catharsis. However, he stresses two central points: forgiveness and union with Christ, especially imitating his humble heart. In reference to the first, Isaiah the prophet had already stressed that only repentance and God's forgiveness could cleanse the heart. He said in God's name, "Wash yourselves; make yourselves clean . . . cease to do evil, learn to do good . . . though your sins are like scarlet, they shall be as white as snow" (1:16–18).

Jesus takes up this forgiveness theme in a detailed parable in Matthew 18:21–35. Peter had asked him, "Lord, how often shall my brother sin against me, and I forgive him? As many as seven times?" Jesus replied to him, "I do not say to you seven times, but seventy times seven." The parable concerns a king (representing God) to whom a servant owed an enormous debt which he could not possibly repay even in a lifetime. He deserved the most severe punishment, yet he entreated the king and was granted full forgiveness of the debt. However, the ungrateful servant had a fellow worker who owed him a relatively trivial amount. Despite his companion's pleas for mercy, the servant had him thrown into prison until all the money was repaid. Upon hearing this, the king ordered the servant to be severely punished. The parable ends with the words, "So also will my heavenly Father do to every one of you, if you do not forgive your brother *from your heart*."

This forgiveness *from the heart* is total, complete and merciful, for it is a response to and imitation of God's own forgiveness. It is interesting that the central prayer of Christianity, taught by Jesus, has the words, "Forgive us our trespasses as we *have forgiven* those who trespass against us" (6:12), The Greek uses the perfect tense, not the present. The Revised Standard translation preserves this translation. It implies that we must make a real heart catharsis by removing hatred from our hearts so they can be open to receiving God's loving action and forgiveness.

In regard to the second area of application, union with Christ, Matthew preserves Jesus' words:

> Come to me, all you who labor and are heavy-laden, and I will give you rest. Take my yoke upon you, and learn from me; for I am gentle and lowly in heart, and you will find rest for your souls. For my yoke is easy, and my burden is light (11:28–30).

Note the focus of imitation on the heart of Christ as gentle and lowly. The words "Come to me" sum up what Matthew has been presenting throughout his Gospel: that Jesus' followers should come to him personally in obedience and faith to learn a new way of life from him. It is a way of love and gentleness as typified by the image of his gentle and humble heart. Later we will see much more on Christ's heart when we come to John's Gospel.

Exercises and Suggested Applications

The best exercise and application is that suggested by Matthew himself in relating the above story of Jesus. Jesus' parables were meant to be an ideal instrument for self-identification and healing. After some minutes of conscious breathing exercise for relaxation, imagine (with closed eyes if that helps you) that you, in place of Peter, are asking the question, "Lord, how often shall my brother sin against me, and I forgive him? As many as seven times?" Then think of some occasion that may still bother you—a time when you have hurt someone else, or he or she has hurt you. Hear Jesus reply to you in these words, "I do not say to you seven times but seventy times seven." Trust in these words—that if Jesus gives you this difficult challenge, he will also give you the strength to respond to it.

In the parable, imagine that you are the servant whom God the king has forgiven an enormous debt. Recall the many occasions when God has lifted from your shoulders the heavy burden of guilt and sadness. You deserved just punishment but instead God has lavished his forgiveness and love upon you. Contrast how small the hurt you have experienced is in relation to the offenses you have given to your Creator. A great gift of healing is needed, so listen to Jesus' words, "Come to me, all who labor and are heavy-laden, and I will give you rest. . . . Learn of me, for I am gentle and lowly in *heart*" (11:28–29). Draw close to this loving heart.

Keeping the heart focus, imagine the time Peter denied three times, even on oath, that he never knew Christ, and yet Jesus turned his eyes and heart to him. It was this grace that made Peter so thoroughly change that he became the rock of Christ's Church. Recall the sadness of Jesus' heart on being betrayed by Judas, one of the twelve who even shared all of Jesus' meals. Jesus received the most cruel blow a human being could experience, yet there was forgiveness and love for Judas in his heart. Try to identify with this loving, compassionate, and forgiving heart of Christ.

Recall now Jesus' closing words in the parable about forgiving from the heart. Focus your breathing on your heart area, and keep saying to yourself in regard to the hurt you have experienced: "I forgive you from my heart." Repeat this phrase until you feel it deep in your heart. Repeat the exercise if negative or hostile feelings arise again. In this exercise it is important to fully experience in your body all the feelings that may come to the surface so that they may be fully healed and transformed.

9
Luke and the One Heart
in God and Humanity

Luke is the most "heart-conscious" writer in the New Testament. In his Gospel, he uses the word some twenty-four times, more than any other evangelist. In his second volume, the Acts of the Apostles, the heart is mentioned another twenty-one times, for a total of forty-five. This does not count important equivalents which we shall point out. We shall concentrate our study on the meaning areas that are unique or especially characteristic of Luke. These (with some overlapping) are the following:

◊ The one heart of God
◊ The heart in repentance, decision and change
◊ The pondering heart and scriptural reflection
◊ The heart in remembrance and memory

Luke and the One Heart of God

An important key to Luke, as it was with Matthew, is the central confession of faith, the Jewish *Shemah*. In Matthew, we saw that the *second* commandment was *like* the first. However, in Luke, there is no second commandment but only one. When a lawyer tested Jesus, inquiring what he should do to inherit eternal life, Jesus asked him what was written in the law. The lawyer responded:

> You shall love the Lord your God with all your heart and with all your soul and with all your strength and with all your mind, *and your neighbor as yourself* (10:25–27).

Jesus agreed with the lawyer's statement and said to him, "Do this and you shall live" (10:28). We immediately note that in Luke's version there is no separation or addition in regard to love of neighbor. They form one commandment. To make sure the message is unmistakable, Luke follows this with the story of the Good Samaritan who demonstrated this type of love and thus showed he loved God as well. We will study the significance of this parable further on in this chapter.

Right from the first chapter of his Gospel, Luke points out the origins of all love in the universe. Zechariah predicts that his son John the Baptist will go before the Lord to prepare his way and give knowledge of salvation to his people through forgiveness of sins. This will come as a result of the "tender mercy" of God which will shine on the darkness of the world like the rays of the rising sun (1:77–79).

The Greek words behind the English translation "tender mercy" are *splagchna eleous*. In Greek, *splagchna* refers to the inner human parts: heart, liver, lungs, etc., and, by extension, the womb. Similarly, and often parallel to the heart, it is the seat of the deepest emotions. For example, in the Book of Wisdom it is the source of Abraham's love for his son Isaac (10:5). In the Fourth Book of Maccabees (14:13) it is the place where a mother feels the love for her child. As applied to God, the two Greek words go back to the Hebrew *rahamei hesed*. In Chapter 2 we saw this first word as derived from the root *rehem* or womb, as the first place where God's love, *hesed,* is at work in human beings. In Jewish literature not long before the time of Jesus, the same Lukan Greek phrase for "tender mercy" is found in the Testament of Zebulun, where the revelation of this "tender mercy" is reserved for the last days (8:2). In other books, the Messiah is identified with the "tender mercy" of God (Test. Naphtali 4:5; Test. Levi 4:4). There is, however, some possibility of later Christian interpolation in these Jewish documents. There is no doubt however, that Luke considered God's wombal compassion/mercy behind these Greek words.

This special compassionate love begins with God and then is mirrored through Jesus, who teaches it to his disciples. In the parable of the prodigal son, the gracious forgiving father (who represents God) reflects this loving quality:

> While he was yet at a distance, his father saw him and had compassion (*esplagchnisthē*) and ran and embraced him and kissed him (15:20).

Jesus, the Lord, is described as possessing the same divine quality when he meets the widow of Naim who suffered the loss of her only son, and then raises him to life (7:13). Then the Samaritan stranger is an instrument of the same womb/compassion when he sees by the roadside a Jew who was beaten by robbers and lay half dead:

> But a Samaritan, as he journeyed, came to where he was; and when he saw him, he had compassion (same word as 7:13; 15:20), and went to him and bound up his wounds, pouring on oil and wine; then he set him on his own beast and brought him to an inn, and took care of him (10:34).

Thus Luke has effectively illustrated the teaching of Jesus in regard to the one commandment by showing that there is only one love of God that exists in the world. Jesus is an instrument of this, and so is anyone who shows the same compassion to those in need. This love has its origin in the maternal heart-beat experience of the womb as the first place where God's action and love are experienced.

To "Turn the Heart"
—Decision, Repentance and Change

Luke knew well the last words of the last written prophet in the Bible, Malachi, who announced that the great reformer Elijah would return before "the great and terrible day of the Lord to turn the hearts of fathers to their children and the hearts of children to their fathers" (4:5–6). Luke calls attention to this "turning of the heart" in the beginning of his Gospel when the angel Gabriel announces to Zechariah the birth of a future son, John the Baptist. The angel says that John "will go before him (the Lord) in the spirit and power of Elijah to turn the hearts of the fathers to the children and the disobedient to the wisdom of the just, to make ready for the Lord a people prepared" (1:7). As we have noted, this will begin the process of forgiveness of sins through the "tender mercy" of God (1:77). Luke notes the fulfillment of Malachi's prophecy as John the Baptist preaches near the Jordan River and announces a "baptism of repentance for the forgiveness of sins" (3:3).

Luke emphasizes that the heart is the place where this decision for repentance must begin. He develops this theme in Jesus' seed parable. In Luke's version, "the seed is the word of God" (8:11). This word of God goes out to the world, but "the devil comes and takes the word from their hearts, that they may not believe and be saved" (8:12). In contrast, the seed falling on receptive and open hearts is described as follows:

> As for that in the good soil, they are those who, hearing
> the word, hold it fast in an honest and upright heart, and
> bring forth fruit with patience (8:15).

The very last words of Jesus in Luke's Gospel direct that "repentance and forgiveness of sins should be preached in his name to all nations beginning with Jerusalem" (24:47). Luke's second volume describes how the early Church followed Jesus' directions and acted through him. On Pentecost Day, Peter preached to the assembled crowds after the Spirit of Jesus had descended upon the apostles. Their reaction is noted as follows, "They were cut to the heart" (2:37). St. Paul continued in the same way. The Gospel first came to Europe when Paul preached to a group of women near a river in Philippi, Macedonia. One of the listeners was a prominent wealthy woman called Lydia who had her own extensive household. Luke notes, "The Lord opened her *heart* to give heed to what was said by Paul" (16:14). Thus Paul's message is not a not a mere human word, but God's action in the human heart.

   As the Gospel of Luke ended with Jesus' injunction to preach repentance, so also Luke's second volume, the Acts of the Apostles, ends with an announcement that the command of Jesus has been fulfilled. The result of preaching has been a time for decision for many people, showing where their hearts are, quoting the prophecy of Isaiah with its double reference to the heart:

> This people's heart has grown dull, and their ears are
> heavy of hearing and their eyes they have closed: lest
> they should perceive with their eyes, and hear with their

ears, and understand with their heart, and turn to me to heal them (Is 6:9–10).

The Pondering Heart and Scriptural Reflection

The central issue for Luke's Gospel is the death of Jesus and its impact. Luke's audience knew well that a Roman execution on the cross was reserved for the most horrible crimes, for traitors and for revolutionaries. It was an unforgettable public disgrace for any family to have someone who underwent this punishment. It marked the crucified one as a complete "loser" and failure in every possible way. What about the death of Jesus on the cross and Christians who followed the same path? It was supremely important for Luke to show how God could transform the shame of a crucifixion into a glorious triumph. It would be God's greatest miracle, if somehow he could be victorious despite the lowest point of human weakness—if he could accomplish the world's salvation by turning upside down all ordinary human standards of success.

However, the reversal of the cross could only be brought about if somehow this supreme disgrace was already in the plan of God found in the Scriptures. It could be no accident or unforeseen happening; otherwise it would be due to human workings. Consequently, Luke is concerned throughout his Gospel to show that Jesus' suffering and death is not a cruel mistake but actually God's own chosen means to save the world as found in his mysterious hidden plan in the Scriptures.

Right from the very first verse of his Gospel, Luke tells us that he will write about the "things fulfilled among us." In these words, he has in mind the great plan of God in the Scriptures as fulfilled in the events of Jesus' ministry, espe-

cially in the scandal of the cross. Luke wants to point this out
so his readers may be assured of the certainty of the Christian instruction they have received. Accordingly, since the
heart is the center of God's action in us, Luke concentrates
his attention on the pondering heart as the central locale for
understanding God's plan in the Scriptures.

As a model for the "pondering heart" in regard to the divine plan, Luke presents Mary the Mother of Jesus as a
model for believing. Twice the evangelist mentions that
Mary pondered over words in her heart (2:19, 51). In the
first case it is over shepherds' report of the angelic message
that the child would be the Davidic Messiah and Lord promised by the Scriptures (2:10). In the second case she keeps in
her heart the words of the young Jesus in the temple when he
announced that he must be about the "things of his Father."
The story of the shocking three day loss of the child Jesus parallels the end of the Gospel, and is a hint that Mary keeps in
mind Jesus' words despite the suffering caused her. She be-
lieves even though she does not understand. A shadow of
the cross is also found in the prediction of Simeon that the
child will be a sign of contradiction and that a sword will
pierce her inner spirit (2:34–35).

The expression that Jesus' Mother "kept all these words
in her heart" is very similar to the Book of Daniel where the
prophet states: "I kept the whole matter (or word) in my
heart" (7:28). There are a number of striking parallels between Daniel and Mary. The same angel Gabriel announces
the message to each of them, the only places in the Bible
where this angel is mentioned (Lk 1:19, 26; Dn 8:16; 9:21;
10:12). The message in both cases is about the interpretation
of Scripture and the coming kingdom. In Daniel, the
prophet searches to understand the hidden divine plan in the
Scriptures of Jeremiah and the angel brings him the interpre-

tation (9:1–27). It is an interpretation that will involve God's victory only after terrible suffering that will include the destruction of Jerusalem and the closing of the temple (9:24–27). So a comparison between Daniel and Mary seems intended by Luke, who presents her as a model of pondering over the divine plan in the Scriptures, even though it may mean terrible suffering before God's victory comes about.

In the rest of his Gospel, Luke continues the same theme of the cross in God's hidden scriptural plan. He does this through Jesus' three predictions that his suffering, death and resurrection *must* take place. While Mark and Matthew indicate the mysterious nature of these sayings, Luke underlines the hiddenness and human incomprehensibility more than the other Gospels do. At the end of the second prediction, Matthew simply notes that the disciples were greatly distressed (17:23). Mark writes that they did not understand the saying (9:32). However, Luke adds the following: "It was concealed from them, that they should not perceive it" (9:45). The evangelist emphasizes this hiddenness because he is convinced that God's mysterious plan to save people through the shame of the cross is so completely beyond human minds that it only can be revealed by the risen Jesus (24:25–27, 32, 45).

Remembrance, Memory and "Burning Hearts"

In our previous study of heart language, we have already seen that the heart is the great instrument of memory. After the crucifixion, it will only be the risen Jesus or his Spirit that will be able to enlighten the disciples and enable them to recall Jesus' words and the meaning of the divine plan in the Scriptures. This will be brought out in Luke's sto-

ries of the empty tomb and the apparitions of the risen Jesus
in his final chapter (Lk 24).

First of all the "two men" at the empty tomb tell Mary
Magdalene and the others, "*Remember* how he told you,
while he was still in Galilee, that the Son of Man must be delivered into the hands of sinful men, and be crucified, and on
the third day rise" (24:5). Luke draws attention to the moment of enlightenment with the expression, "And they remembered his words." Following this, the women, as the
first messengers of the resurrection, went to tell the others.

In a second apparition, two disciples leaving Jerusalem
for Emmaus meet a mysterious stranger who later reveals
himself as the risen Jesus. The fellow-traveler asks them
what they had been discussing together on the journey. They
tell him about the recent events in Jerusalem, how Jesus had
been condemned and crucified despite their hopes that he
would be the one to redeem Israel (24:13–21). Then the dis-
guised risen Christ says to them, "O foolish men and slow of
heart to believe all that the prophets have spoken! Was it not
necessary that the Christ should suffer these things and enter
into his glory?" (24:26). Then the stranger went on to describe all the Scriptures and prophets that spoke of him, and
interpreted them.

The essential place of the heart in this whole matter is
emphasized when Jesus reveals himself to his disciples during the breaking of bread at the inn where they stayed. After
they recognized Jesus and he vanished from their sight, they
said to one another, "Did not our hearts burn within us while
he talked to us on the road, while he opened to us the Scriptures?" (24:32). The connection of this breaking of bread
with remembrance is significant, because the meaning of
bread is central for Luke. The early Church meets together
and prays on this occasion (Acts 2:46; 20:7, where it is on

Sunday, the first day of the week as in Lk 24:1). These texts are no doubt linked with Luke's Last Supper account toward which the whole Gospel seems to be moving. We have mentioned the strong remembrance theme of the supper of the Lord with Luke's longer Greek version having the words, "Do this in remembrance of me" (22:19; cf. 1 Cor 11:25). Also Luke's mention of the new covenant in the Last Supper narrative is a link with Jeremiah's use of the expression "new covenant" in his new heart-covenant text of 31:31 which we discussed in Chapter 5.

Reflections and Exercise

The scandal of the cross was not a popular topic in Luke's time, nor is it so today. It is a "loser" theology, and who wants to be a loser? Yet, in the divine plan, Jesus had to lose in order to win, and Luke's Gospel more than any other brings out the frightful cost of discipleship. All the Gospels have Jesus' word about taking up the cross and following him, but Luke gives special stress to it by adding the word "daily," so we have the following, "If any one would come after me, let that person deny himself, take up his cross *daily* and follow me" (9:23).

For most people, the hope of "winning" provides daily excitement and makes life interesting. This winning may be a sports event, a success in some way, an advance in salary, or prestige, a promotion, beating others in competition, etc. Some of this "winning" may simply be the development of our natural talents and the sense of achievment that comes from doing so. However, there is much evidence that "winning" so dominates some people's lives that they sacrifice their ideals and values in order to "win." At times, so much time must be given over to the quest of "winning" that little time is left for the way Luke points out to follow Jesus.

Luke would have us deliberately ask ourselves, "What are the areas in my life where I can deliberately choose to be a "loser" in order to keep my ideals, or to obtain more time for God's kingdom? And if I choose to be a "loser," what is there left to motivate me in this competitive modern world? How will I spend my time? Luke provides an answer to these questions in his presentation of Jesus' ideal of a life of loving service to others. At the Last Supper story in Luke, the disciples were arguing over this very matter of "winning" by having important positions of authority. Jesus answered,

> But not so with you: rather let the greatest among you become as the youngest, and the leader as one who serves. For which is the greater, one who sits at table, or one who serves? Is it not the one who sits at table? But I am among you as one who serves (22:26–27).

For Luke, Jesus' new heart covenant meal of the Last Supper is a remembrance meal that prompts the disciple to become another Christ by a life of loving service to others. Oneness with Christ, by taking his bread/body, means having the same compassionate love by which he served others. We can see then why Luke only writes of one commandment. Loving God means reflecting his *rahum,* his compassionate heart/womb love to others, as the Samaritan did when he "stopped business," became a loser and rescued a dying man by the road, even assuming any future bills that might be incurred from the man's medical treatment and cure: "Take care of him: and whatever more you spend, I will repay you when I come back" (10:35). The concluding words of Jesus are a challenge for us at any time: "Go and do likewise" (10:37).

10

The Fourth Gospel, the Beloved Disciple and the Heart of Christ

No one has ever seen God; (God) the only Son, who is in the bosom of the Father, he has made him known (1:18).

These words introduce a central theme in the Gospel of John: Jesus is the only one who has completely known the deep inner love of God; his mission on earth is to reveal this to others so they too can have the same experience. The words "no one has ever seen God" recall Chapter 2 where we saw that Moses begged God to let him see his face, but God replied that no one could possibly see him and then continue living (Ex 33:20). God, however, granted Moses a partial glimpse by revealing his name as he passed by. On this occasion, God pronounced his great name, explaining it by the first attribute of his *rachum* (Ex 33:6) or womb compassion, because of its special manifestation in the maternal heartbeat experience. Jesus' mission to the world is to reveal this love to human beings, especially his disciples.

The Gospel writer has had a deep experience of this manifestation of God's love in Jesus, and wants to make it known to his audience. He announces that he has been a chosen witness: "We have beheld his glory, glory as of the only Son from the Father" (1:14). The word "glory" in the Bible always refers to some visible manifestation of God that is perceptible to human beings. The writer wants to tell others what he has seen and experienced in such a way that it will be a model for them also. Therefore he chooses to make himself anonymous in the Gospel by referring to himself as the "disciple whom Jesus loved," so that others may identify with him, and place themselves in the texts.

The title "beloved disciple" also authenticates a special role that the writer has played in Jesus' life that gives him a unique authority for his audience. The role of the beloved disciple and his personal experience are often so intermingled that we cannot separate them, and perhaps he did not separate them himself. The best way to begin understanding him is to look at the principal texts where he describes himself. He calls himself the "other disciple, the one whom Jesus loved" on the occasion when he and Peter ran to verify the empty tomb (20:2). At the foot of the cross, he is "the disciple whom Jesus loved" (19:26). At the Last Supper, he is "one who was at the bosom of Jesus, the one whom Jesus loved" (13:23). There seems to be a special importance to this place at Jesus' bosom, for the description is repeated carefully two verses later where he is described as leaning back on Jesus' chest and asking the question about Judas that Peter had requested. Also, in John 21, the place at Jesus' side is again emphasized as he is called the disciple who reclined at Jesus' breast at the supper (21:20). In the same chapter, the one who recognizes Jesus in the miraculous draught is called the disciple whom Jesus loved (21:7).

What did the author mean by these two descriptions, first as beloved disciple, and, second, at the bosom of Jesus? In biblical fashion, let us take the second term, bosom, first. The Greek word *kolpos* refers to the whole heart region or chest. The evangelist uses *kolpos* in all the texts above except in 13:25 and 21:10 where he has *stethos,* chest, in parallel to *kolpos.* There seems to be a direct parallel to the opening text in 1:18, where Jesus learns about the inner secrets of God's compassionate/womb love at the bosom of his Father. Jesus' relationship to his Father is paralleled by the disciple's relation to Jesus. This parallel is found elsewhere in the Gospel. Jesus says at the Last Supper, "As the Father has loved me, so have I loved you: abide in my love" (13:24). Jesus' last words and prayer to his Father before the passion story are, "I have made known to them your name, and I will make it known, that the love with which you have loved me may be in them, and I in them." So the position at the bosom of Jesus indicates not only the author's special privilege to understand Jesus' love, but the place where any disciple can come to learn about God's love.

The expression "disciple or one whom Jesus loved" has a very similar meaning, and is almost a parallel. The very meaning of a disciple is "one whom Jesus loves." In regard to other persons, the same expression is used. Thus Lazarus is called "he whom you love" (11:3). Likewise the Gospel relates, "Jesus loved Martha and her sister and Lazarus" (11:5). Thus in both expressions, our author is one who has a special place close to Jesus so he can personally experience God's love manifest in his teacher. At the same time, his role is representative, so it can stand for any sincere believer.

In addition, the author seems to have had a deeper meaning in mind if we look at the Old Testament background of the words. This has been pointed out in Paul Minear's[21] study of the beloved disciple in the Fourth Gospel. He has called attention to the remarkable similarities to Benjamin, the favorite and beloved son of Jacob/Israel. The touching story of the very close relationship between Jacob and Benjamin is found in Genesis. Benjamin's mother Rachel had died in childbirth. After his brother Joseph had been sold into Egypt, the father-son relation of Jacob and Benjamin became so strong that the Bible states that the father's life was so bound up with the boy that if anything happened to him he would die (44:30). Minear also states that the most significant text is that found in Deuteronomy 33:1–26 where Moses gives his last testament and final blessing to the tribes of Israel. There Benjamin is signaled out in a special manner:

> Of Benjamin he said, "The beloved of the Lord, he dwells in safety by him: he encompasses him all the day long, and makes his dwelling between his shoulders" (33:12).

In the above text, Benjamin is indeed marked out as a very special and favorite son. He is the beloved, *ēgapēmenos* (Greek Old Testament). According to the Greek, "he rested between his (God's) shoulders," just as the beloved disciple rested on the bosom of Jesus. The text appears in a final blessing of Moses, so this would give a special authority to Benjamin and place him in a unique place as a successor of Jacob as a favorite son. This authority would be very important for the beloved disciple as a witness to his community and successor to Jesus in the role of "favorite son." Thus the place at the bosom of Jesus held by the beloved disciple gives him special authority, keeping in mind the parallel to Jacob and Benjamin.

There may be another element connected to this place at the bosom of Jesus which would strengthen the beloved disciple's position. The placing of a child at the bosom is a symbol of adoption. For example, when Ruth in the Old Testament gave birth to a boy, Ruth's mother Naomi adopted him as her own in place of her own sons who had died. She did this by formally taking the child and placing it in her bosom. This was officially recognized by her neighbors who said, "A son has been born to Naomi" (4:11–17).

Jesus' call of the beloved disciple confirms his very special place as favorite son of Jesus and model for believers. Jesus' words here are his first in this Gospel and set the tone for much that is to follow. It is John the Baptist himself who introduces two of his disciples to Jesus by looking at him passing nearby and announcing, "Behold the Lamb of God" (1:35). This statement is central for the Gospel, so it is here repeated a second time. John the Baptist had earlier identified Jesus publicly with the words, "Behold the Lamb of God who takes away the sin of the world!" (1:29). Only Andrew, brother of Peter, is identified by name as one of the two disciples. However, there are significant parallels between this "Lamb of God" introduction and the foot of the cross where the writer as the beloved disciple identifies Jesus as the paschal lamb by pointing to the fulfillment of the Scriptures of the paschal lamb ritual, "Not a bone of his shall be broken" (19:36). These parallels make it likely that the other disciple with Andrew was the beloved disciple.

> The two disciples heard him say this and they followed Jesus. Jesus turned, and saw them following, and said to them, "What do you seek?" And they said to him, "Rabbi" (which means Teacher), "where are you staying?" He said to them, "Come and see." They came and saw where he was staying: and they stayed with him that day, for it was about the tenth hour (1:37–42).

The author describes no other call in such detail as this first one, so it must have great importance for him and his audience. An important key to its meaning is the word "stay" or "abide," corresponding to the Greek *menein,* a favorite theme in the Gospel of John. The word is repeated three times in this passage, and announces the Gospel theme that Jesus invites disciples to abide with him, just as he abides with the Father and the Spirit manifested at his baptism (1:32–33; 14:10, 17; 15:4, 5, 7, 9, 10).

A permanent abiding seems hinted in this first call. The disciples arrive at the tenth hour, probably about four o'clock, and stay for the day, which would be until the next evening in the biblical way of counting days. The expression "for the day" can symbolize a much longer period. The action of Jesus can be better understood in terms of hospitality customs of the time. Jesus invites them into his own abode, which is tantamount to inviting them to be considered as members of his own family. What Jesus does for the two disciples, he later does for all at the Last Supper in the hospitality and welcoming action of washing the feet.

The passage previously discussed about Benjamin the beloved son (Deut 33:12) may be in the background for our understanding of the text. There it is a question of God's permanent abiding presence with the beloved son "all day long," just as in the Gospel text. The Greek Old Testament translates "all day long" as "always," which strengthens our interpretation above. All in all, the call of the beloved disciple strengthens the portrait of a beloved, adopted son of Jesus, who stands as a model for any believer who is called to God's sonship: "To all who received him, who believed in his name, he gave power to become children of God" (1:12).

Beloved Disciple and Beloved Disciples

However, the readers of this Gospel are not able to meet Jesus, stay in his home and recline at his bosom like the beloved disciple. How are they to obtain the same privileged position? Jesus points to the cross as the means by which he will draw everyone to himself: "I when I am lifted up will draw everyone to myself" (12:32). Consequently, the author focuses special attention to the dramatic events he has witnessed at the foot of the cross. This is especially true of the unusual flow of blood and water from Jesus' side:

> One of the soldiers pierced his side with a spear, and at once there came out blood and water. He who saw it has borne witness—and he knows that he tells the truth—that you also may believe. For these things took place that the Scripture might be fulfilled, "Not a bone of his shall be broken." And again another Scripture says, "They shall look on him whom they have pierced" (19:34–37).

The event is so extraordinary for the evangelist because it is a sign that Jesus' promise of the Spirit has been fulfilled through an obedient sacrificial death like that of the Jewish paschal lamb that has opened up God's forgiveness and mercy to the world.

First of all, in regard to the promise of the Spirit, our author has in mind Jesus' striking words at the Jewish feast of Booths:

> On the last day of the feast, the great day, Jesus stood up and proclaimed, "If anyone thirst, let him come to me and drink—he who believes in me as the Scripture has said, 'Out of his heart shall flow rivers of living water.' " Now this he said about the Spirit, which those who believed in him were to receive; for as yet the Spirit had not been given, because Jesus was not yet glorified (7:37–39).

Since the author believed that God was behind all such extraordinary events, the flow of blood and water was an indication that Jesus had fulfilled his promise that water/Spirit would proceed from within him to believers. (While some Greek texts indicate that the Spirit proceeds from the believer, the whole Gospel context points rather to Jesus as the source of the Spirit.) The expression "from his heart" corresponds to the Greek, "from his belly" (*koilia*), which means the heart and inner parts. It thus parallels the watery blood flowing from the side of Christ. The actual flow was important for sacrifice as P. Ellis reminds us in his book, *The Genius of John.*[22]

The second part, fulfillment of Scriptures, was equally important for the writer. Jesus' death, like every sacrifice, had to be in complete voluntary obedience to God if it was to be effective. The unusual flow from Jesus' side reminded the beloved disciple that the Scriptures about the paschal lamb were also fulfilled. And this was also a fulfillment of the double announcement of John the Baptist that Jesus was the "Lamb of God who takes away the sins of the world" (1:29, 36). An important regulation for the paschal lamb sacrifice was that no bone should be broken (Ex 12:46). Here again the author considered it quite unusual that the soldiers would break the bones of those crucified with Jesus to make sure they were dead, and yet would not do the same for Jesus (19:33). Jesus' entire obedience to his Father until the last moment is brought out by his acceptance of sour wine "to fulfill the Scripture" (19:28; Ps 69:21). Jesus' last words, "It is finished (or completed)," signify his complete obedience to God's plan until his last breath when he bowed his head and "gave up his spirit" (19:30). The use of this last phrase may have the deeper meaning that Jesus released the divine Spirit to believers as a result of his obedient death.

We have seen that Jesus' death makes it possible for every believer to have the same relationship to Jesus as the beloved disciple. Every "beloved disciple" can reach to the same source within Jesus' bosom, the Spirit of love. Yet, how can he or she do this? The answer is provided in Jesus' first sign at Cana in Galilee, which very much complements the events at the cross. On the cross, it was Jesus' perfect obedience, even to drinking the sour wine foretold by the Scriptures, that made his death the vehicle of the Spirit. At Cana, it is the disciples' obedience to Jesus' word, like Jesus' obedience to the Father, that makes possible the new wine of the Spirit.

Looking at the Cana sign, we find the central place[23] of Jesus' Mother there as at the cross. When the wine runs short, she tells her son about it, but he responds that he is not interested in a miracle on the same level of meaning. He looks forward to the cross and says, "My hour has not yet come." Thus the reader is to interpret the miracle in reference to the events at Calvary. Jesus' mother instructs the waiters, "Do whatever he tells you" (2:5). It is carefully noted that the waiters do everything exactly as Jesus orders. She tells them, "Do whatever he tells you" and their complete compliance is noted with the words, "And they filled them up to the brim." He further orders, "Now draw some out, and take it to the steward of the feast." Then the obedient response, "So they took it." As a result, the wedding steward finds that the water is now a new wine reserved for the last part of the feast. Thus we learn that complete obedience to Jesus' word is necessary to receive the new wine of the Spirit. It is the same obedience that Jesus showed to his Father on the cross.

The first step in this obedience is described in the stories of Nicodemus and the Samaritan woman. Jesus told the Jewish teacher who had come to him secretly at night, "Amen, amen, I say to you, unless one is born anew, he cannot see the kingdom of God" (3:3). This birth is further specified as follows, "Unless one is born of water and the

Spirit, he cannot enter the kingdom of God" (3:5). In parallel, Jesus tells the Samaritan woman, "Whoever drinks of the water that I shall give will never thirst; the water that I will give will become a spring of water welling up to eternal life." The symbolism in a new birth with water and the Spirit points to the sacrament of baptism, a first beginning for believers.

However, this is only a start and points to a much more continual experience. When will this happen? The Last Supper scene in John 13–17, with Jesus' final words, points to a central experience in the believers. In these chapters, we find the word "abide" some fifteen times. In addition, it is at the Last Supper that the beloved disciple has his supreme privilege of reclining at the bosom of Jesus. It is twice mentioned—here and then again in 21:20.

However, if this Last Supper is so important, why is there no mention in John's Gospel about Jesus giving himself to his disciples as bread and wine, an event that is so important in Matthew, Mark and Luke as a prelude to Jesus' death? An answer is suggested by studying a well authenticated structure of the signs in the Fourth Gospel drawn up by M. Girard.[24] It is a chiastic structure with the multiplication of the loaves in a central place of the Gospel. The following is the suggested schema:

(1) The wedding feast at Cana (2:1–12)
    (2) The restoration of the dying son (4:46–54)
        (3) The sabbath healing at Bethesda (5:1–16)
            (4) The multiplication of loaves (6:1–71)
        (5) The sabbath healing of the blind man (9:1–41)
    (6) The restoration of Lazarus to life (11:1–44)
(7) The great hour of Jesus: his mother, the cross, and the issue of blood and water from Jesus' side (19:25–37)

We notice immediately how well the structure is inter-connected. Signs two and six concern death to life; three and five are sabbath healings; one and seven complement each other, with the parallels of obedience, wine, water, and the presence of Jesus' Mother. Sign four, the mystery of the loaves, stands in the middle—a central point toward which all the signs point, especially the seventh which shares with the fourth the only mention of Jesus' blood in the Gospel. In the fourth sign are found the notable words of Jesus describing how a believer can permanently abide with him:

> Amen, amen, I say to you, unless you eat the flesh of the Son of Man and drink his blood, you have no life in you; he who eats my flesh and drinks my blood has eternal life, and I will raise him up at the last day. . . . He who eats my flesh and drinks my blood abides in me, and I in him (6:53–56).

As R.E. Brown[25] explains in detail in his commentary on John, these words are equivalent to the Last Supper insti-tution words found in Matthew, Mark and Luke. It is only to have them at a central literary point in his Gospel, to-ward which everything else points, that the author has placed them in the middle, according to his ladder struc-ture.

We can now understand why the beloved disciple is so prominent in the Last Supper in the intimate place, lean-ing on the Lord's bosom, and partaking secrets that no one else knows. He is the figure of every beloved disciple at the eucharistic table. These meetings together are a high point in the abiding presence of Jesus that is central to the Gospel. This is why the crowds, with a hidden double meaning, say to Jesus, "Lord, give us this bread always" (6:34).

Summary

The Fourth Gospel starts with the eternal Son of God at the bosom of his Father sharing his great inner womb-compassion love for all people. Jesus comes on earth to invite others to know this also. The only way is through him. This is illustrated by the beloved disciple who is adopted and chosen as a favorite son of Jesus, like the beloved Benjamin in the Old Testament. Every believer likewise is called to be a beloved disciple. This is made possible by the death of Jesus on the cross. The water and blood from his side symbolize the Spirit he has promised. This Spirit is made possible by his obedient and sacrificial death, like the passover lamb. By obeying Jesus, just as he obeyed his Father to the end, the disciple can likewise come to know God's love in the bosom of Jesus. This obedience begins at baptism by being born anew in water and in Spirit. It is renewed and reaches its highest moments at the eucharistic Lord's supper where the believer, like the beloved disciple, rests on the bosom of Jesus.

Suggestions for Practice

What is so striking about John's Gospel are the personalistic terms in which Christian discipleship is expressed. These terms point to a very definite "feminine side" within every human being. Everything starts from the "feminine" womb/bosom love of God known by Jesus. Then this is exemplified by a "beloved disciple" whose principal delight is his close relationship to Jesus as a favored son. "Reclining in Jesus" is a hardly a "macho" expression that would be favored by competitive sports stars, aggressive business executives, or prestigious academicians. The portrait of the beloved disciple is a challenge to competitive and violent modern society. It prompts all of us to ask the serious question, "Are personal relationships and sensitivity to other human beings *the* priority in my life?" The answer was "yes" for the beloved disciple who found this answer as he reclined on the bosom of Jesus.

This priority of relationships affects the meaning of the Eucharist, which we found to be central for the Fourth Gospel. The Last Supper of Jesus was not just a group get-together, but a community of individuals who had drawn from the same deep source and now could let that flow to others as well. That is why Jesus said at the Last Supper:

> A new commandment I give to you, that you love one another, even as I have loved you, that you also love one another. By this all will know that you are my disciples, if you have love for one another (13:34–35).

11

The Mystery of the Missing Heart
or the Rise and Fall of
"Devotion to the Sacred Heart"

They have taken away my Lord, and I do not know
where they have laid him (Jn 20:13).

These words register the shock and surprise of Mary
Magdalene in not finding the familiar body of the Jesus she
knew so well in the tomb on Easter Sunday. But strangely
enough they were the first words that came to mind of the
old man that morning when he arrived at church for his
morning prayers and meditation. (What follows is a true
story with fictionalized details to conceal the identity of
those involved.)

He entered the church and walked down the right side
past the old confessionals until he came to the favorite side
chapel that he had known since childhood. When he looked
up to pray, he could hardly believe his eyes: the familiar picture of the Sacred Heart was no longer there. Not that he
really needed the external representation: the details were
engraved in his mind from that first moment as a child when

he saw the picture and began to understand what God's love was all about. He could almost see it still there: Jesus' face sorrowful and compassionate, holding his heart in his hand. The heart was encircled with thorns and on fire with love. There were signs of a wound that had pierced his heart and the whole area radiated light. The old man could almost hear the words Jesus was saying, words that had been said to St. Margaret Mary Alacoque and repeated so often in sermons and in school: "Behold the heart that has so loved us that it has spared nothing to be spent and consumed for them to testify its love. And yet in return it has received so much coldness, indifference, and even contempt."

Being a man of action, our visitor looked around the church for the missing image. He finally found it in a corner of the sacristy and feared that it might even be eventually disposed of. He went immediately to the pastor and asked for an explanation. The priest told him that the picture had been removed because it was a distraction to the people during the liturgy, which was a celebration of the people of God. In contrast, the Sacred Heart image was individually oriented, and too sentimental. When other church members found out, a flow of protesting letters arrived at the rectory. The pastor finally restored the picture, but placed a curtain over it that could be drawn during the time of the liturgy.

I have told this story because it illustrates a tremendous change that has taken place in the Catholic Church, especially since Vatican Council II in the mid-1960's. To understand this, it will be necessary to briefly review the development of worship and devotion to the heart of Christ after the biblical era.

In the first centuries after the written Gospels, there was no specific attention given to the heart of Christ. However, in equivalent manner, the pierced side of Christ and his wounds were the frequent focus of meditation and prayer. This was really a follow-up on the Johannine emphasis on the side of Christ and his wounds that we saw in the last chapter. For example, St. Augustine (354–430) writes, "John the Evangelist received a special gift from the Lord, upon whose breast he leaned at supper, by which is signified that he drank in the deepest secrets of the inward Heart."[26] Eusebius, the early Church historian, notes that among the early martyrs in Lyons, around 177 A.D., there was a certain young man called Sanctus who "was strengthened by the spring of living waters that flowed from the heart of Christ."[27] Origen (185–253) wrote, "Now that we have learned that he whom Jesus loved rested on the breast of Jesus, let us so act that we also may be judged worthy of special love; then we too shall rest in the bosom of Jesus."[28] St. Gregory the Great (540–604), the last of the Western Fathers, prepared the way for a later full blossoming of private devotion to the heart of Christ when he wrote this commentary on the Song of Songs:

> "Arise, my love, my sister, and come, my dove, in the clefts of the rock, in the hollow places of the wall." By clefts of the rock I mean the wounds in the hands and feet of Christ hanging freely on the cross. By the hollow places in the wall I mean the wound in his side made by the lance.[29]

Similar to Gregory is Bede the Venerable (672–735), who writes:

> "You have wounded my heart, my sister, my spouse." This word is to be taken simply, for by mentioning the wounded Heart it expresses the greatness of the love of Christ for the Church.[30]

However, it was during the Middle Ages that contemplatives led the way for a future spread of private devotion to the heart of Jesus throughout Europe. Meditating on the wounds of Jesus, St. Anselm (1033–1109) wrote about the side of Christ as follows: "That opening reveals to us the riches of his goodness and the charity of his heart toward us."[31] In Western monastic life, St. Bernard (1090–1153) had great influence through his sermons and writings. Dwelling on the wounds of Christ, he wrote:

> The iron pierced his soul, and his heart has drawn near to us, that no longer should he not know how to compassionate my woes. The secrets of his heart lie open to me through the cloven body; that mighty sacrament of love lies open. . . . Why should not the heart lie open through the wounds?[32]

In Paris, the Augustinian Abbey of St. Victor had great influence at a time when the University of Paris was beginning. Richard of St. Victor wrote the following as part of his commentary on the Canticles' verse, "He shall eat butter and honey":

> If we look at the heart of Christ, there is nothing sweeter, nothing kinder. Nowhere can there be a creature sweeter than his heart; no heart could more abound in joy than his.[33]

In this period, women mystics and visionaries had a great influence in spreading popular devotion to the heart of Christ. Their influence would later culminate with Margaret Mary Alacoque in the seventeenth century. Women were especially attracted to the heart of Christ, because, as we have seen, the heart image has feminine origins in the womb experience of the maternal heart beat. The first recorded mystic revelation of Christ's heart is that of St. Lutgardis (1182–1246). Here we see an account of a mystical exchange of hearts that will be a repeated phenomenon through the centuries. We have already seen the influence of the prophet Ezekiel in thinking in terms of such a heart transplant. Lutgardis' biographer records that she asked Jesus for a better gift, his own heart. And the Lord replied that he wanted *her* heart. So she replied, "So be it, Lord, but take it in such wise that the love of thy Heart may be mingled in the love of mine, and that in thee I may possess thy Heart, at all times secure of thy protection."[34]

Among these women mystics, St. Gertrude had a very wide influence through the publication of her *Revelations* which were especially concerned with the heart of Christ. Here once again, we find the prominent feature of the union of hearts. One of the most prominent of Gertrude's revelations occurred on the feast of St. John (whom she considered to be the beloved disciple). St. John brought her in a vision to the place at Jesus' bosom where he had reclined at the Last Supper. "There, as she felt the constant pulsations of the divine heart and rejoiced exceedingly, she said to the saint, 'Beloved of God, did you not feel these pulsations when you were lying on the Lord's breast at the Last Supper?' 'Yes,' he replied, 'and with such plenitude that liquid does not enter more rapidly into bread than the sweetness of these pleasures penetrated my soul, so that my spirit became more ardent than water under the action of a glowing fire.' "[35]

Another prominent woman mystic, Catherine of Siena, played an important political role at a time when Gregory IX was in Avignon, not Rome, and Europe was threatened by schism over the question of the rightful Pope. On July 10,

1370, she was granted a vision in which Jesus made her drink from his side and then took her heart from her breast and exchanged it with his own.[36] Catherine's *Dialogues* were actually a series of conversations between herself (representing the average person) and the eternal Father, with the heart of Christ as the uniting center between both.

The great religious orders especially led the way in promoting devotion to the heart of Jesus. St. Francis shared with his followers his intimate experience of the stigmata of the five wounds of Jesus on his own body. Anthony of Padua had a tremendous influence through his frequent mention of Jesus' heart in his sermons. St. Bonaventure (1221–1274) was called the "seraphic doctor" because of the spirit of burning love in his sermons inspirited by meditation on the pierced heart of Christ. In the Dominicans, St. Albert the Great (1206–1280), teacher of Thomas Aquinas, was the first to connect devotion to the Sacred Heart with the Eucharist and Blessed Sacrament. Blessed Henry Suso composed a preparation for Holy Communion that taught union with Christ's heart in the Sacrament. Tauler (1300–1361), a noted preacher, had a tremendous effect on people through his heart-mysticism and meditation on the passion of Christ.

By the fifteenth and sixteenth centuries, devotion to the Sacred Heart had "gone public." Books were published with litanies, prayers and practices of devotion. During this time, the *Imitation of Christ* by Thomas a Kempis was widely read with its strong emphasis on imitation of Jesus' heart. He wrote in one of his sermons, "Come to the deep Heart, to the hidden Heart, to the secret Heart, to the Heart of God who opens the door to you."[37] The early Jesuits, especially Peter Canisius, began to make the heart of Jesus the theme of their preaching. This prepared the way for the later role they would assume as the principal propagators of this devotion to the whole Catholic world.

The seventeenth century witnessed a continued spread of devotion to Jesus' heart. This was spurred on by a reaction to the Protestant Reformation movement, and a response to the reforms initiated by the Council of Trent. In this period, St. Francis de Sales (1567–1622) had a wide influence through his preaching and writing, especially his *Treatise on the Love of God,* which became a popular manual for spiritual growth that was used for centuries. Pope Pius IX made him a doctor of the Church two hundred years later, mentioning his role in sowing "the seeds of this devotion to the Sacred Heart, which, in these unhappy times, we have the great joy of seeing marvelously spread, to the great profit of religion."

Especially significant in view of the future Margaret Mary Alacoque was Francis' foundation of The Sisters of the Visitation in 1602. He described this congregation as "the work of the Hearts of Jesus and Mary" and designed its coat of arms as a "single Heart pierced with two arrows and surrounded by a crowth of thorns, this Heart serving as the base of a cross that will surmount it and on which will be graven the sacred names of Jesus and Mary."[38] Here we find the image of the heart encircled by thorns, with a cross atop, that would be part of the great popular image of the Sacred Heart in the following centuries.

While private devotion increased during this time, nourished by many books and notable preachers, a significant step took place through the work of St. John Eudes (1601–1680), a member of the Congregation of the Oratory. He composed a Mass and Office in honor of the Sacred Heart. This meant that private devotion could now be linked with official liturgy and thus obtain a much firmer position within the Church.

The way was thus prepared for the final and most important intervention of St. Margaret Mary Alacoque.

Margaret Mary Alacoque (1647–1690) entered the Visitation Sisters in 1671 at their convent in Paray-Le-Monial. Like St. Gertrude before her, she experienced a vision at the feast of St. John in 1673 while praying before the Blessed Sacrament. She described it in this way in her autobiography:

> Our Lord said to me: "My divine Heart is so passionately in love with men that it can no longer withhold the flames of that burning love; it must needs let them spread abroad by means of you, and reveal itself to men to enrich them with its profound treasures which hold the graces they need to be saved from eternal loss. . . ."
> He then asked for my heart, which I begged him to take; he did so, and placed it within his own adorable Heart, in which he showed it to me like a tiny atom being consumed in that burning hearthfire. Then, drawing it out like a glowing flame in the form of a heart, he gave it back to me, saying, "See, my beloved, it is a precious pledge of my love. I will place within your side a little spark of the mighty flame of my love, to serve you for a heart, and to consume you until your last moment."[39]

However, the most influential vision was the so-called "Great Promise" which was given her on June 16, 1675. This paved the way for a dominant place of the Sacred Heart cult in Catholic life and worship. Again her own words:

> He said, "Behold this Heart that has so loved men that it has spared nothing even to exhausting and consuming itself in order to show them its love. And in return from most men I receive only ingratitude, by their irreverences and sacrileges, and by the coldness and contempt which they show to me in this Sacrament of love. But

what wounds me yet more deeply is that this is done by
souls who are consecrated to me."[40]

Then Jesus asked that a special feast of the Sacred Heart be
established, and that Communion be offered up on that day
in reparation for offenses given to his heart. The establishment of this feast by Pope Clement XIII in 1729 ensured a
prominent place for the Sacred Heart in the worship and liturgy of the Catholic Church.

However, popular interest spread like wildfire when the
"promises of the Sacred Heart" became known. The source
of these was a letter written by Margaret Mary to a friend
and brought to light (in a copy only) after her death. Origi-
nally, Jesus had asked Margaret Mary in a vision during 1674
to receive Communion each First Friday of the month in
reparation to his Sacred Heart. Due to Jansenistic influence,
Communion was relatively rare in those days, so such a practice would be unusual. However, in the later "letter," we
have an account of Jesus' special promise that anyone who
made the Nine First Fridays would be assured of the grace of
final salvation.

Margaret Mary's revelations quickly became known to
the general public through her confessor, Claude la Colom-
biere, and other Jesuits. After her death, all of France was
deeply moved by the story of the deliverance of Marseilles
and southern France from the plague through consecration
to the Sacred Heart. Churches became jammed with communicants on the Nine First Fridays as popular enthusiasm
spread in the Church.

Official Church approval gave new impetus to the movement and placed it on a firmer foundation. In 1794, Pope
Pius VI condemned the errors of Jansenism and defended devotion to the heart of Jesus. Pius IX in 1856 completed the
previous work of Clement XIII by extending the feast of the

Sacred Heart to the universal Church and giving it special rank. The work of Margaret Mary was officially sealed when she was beatified in 1864. In 1873, the French National Assembly, after the disastrous Franco-Prussian war, approved a national vow to build a basilica of the Sacred Heart at Montmartre. It was there that the global church was consecrated to the Heart of Christ with the approval of Pius IX. Leo XIII in 1899 extended this action by consecrating the whole human race to the Sacred Heart with a prayer that was to be repeated annually in all churches. In the early 1900's, Pius X ordered a triple invocation, "Most Sacred Heart of Jesus, have mercy on us," to be recited at the end of each Mass.

An encyclical letter of Pius XI in 1925 placed a final official seal on devotion to the Sacred Heart. This was followed by other letters in 1928 and 1932. In 1944, Pope Pius XII aproved the Apostleship of Prayer whose goal was a worldwide extension of the kingdom of God through prayer and reparation to the Sacred Heart. In the papal letter of approval, he wrote that the Apostolate of Prayer "centers their whole-hearted attention on the excellent devotion to the Sacred Heart of Jesus: that devotion in which is contained 'the epitome of our holy religion and of a more perfect way of life.' "

What did all of this mean in Catholic life? Having been in grammar and high school during the late 1930's, my memories are very vivid about this period. In our Catholic school, there was a special Mass for the whole school each First Friday, with special opportunities for confessions beforehand. At the Mass there was a sermon on the Sacred Heart, followed by Benediction and devotions to the Sacred Heart. All day there was exposition of the Blessed Sacrament and we were invited to pick a half-hour when we could pray and meditate in the chapel. On this day, the monthly leaflets of the Apostleship of Prayer were distributed to all the students along with a special intention for the month that could be added to our daily "morning offering." This offering was a special way of dedicating all the events of each day to God through the Sacred Heart in union with the offering of Jesus on the cross, renewed in each Mass. Its words linger in my memory never to be forgotten: "O Jesus, through the most pure heart of Mary, I offer you all my thoughts, words, sufferings and acts of this day for all the intentions of thy most Sacred Heart, in union with all the Masses offered throughout the world."

What was done in the schools was echoed in each parish. Long lines waited to go to confession on the Thursday evening before each First Friday. Many Masses were scheduled for early Friday morning to accommodate the crowds who wished to fulfill the Nine First Fridays (and even repeat them many times) in accord with the "Great Promise" made to St. Margaret Mary. Every church had exposition of the Blessed Sacrament all day. Everyone who could do so stopped by for at least a few moments of prayer. The morning offering and Sacred Heart devotion reached its climax in each Mass where private prayer dominated during the silent Latin Mass. Communicants returned to their places and buried their heads in their hands for fervent personal communication with the heart of Christ, bringing their petitions and anxieties to him.

Devotion to the Sacred Heart continued to hold its central place in Catholic devotion and worship until the 1960's and the profound changes brought about by Vatican Council II. The Council documents made no mention at all of the heart of Jesus. The liturgical document emphasized the Eucharist as the gathering place of the people of God. The teachings on the Eucharist and the Mass focused on community participation, rather than on individual union with

Christ. As a result, Church teaching, practice and education followed the Vatican leadership. Devotion to the Sacred Heart was criticized as being too individualistic, and even sentimental. Official catechisms made no mention of the Sacred Heart, and thus children no longer received early formation in this devotion. Gradually, statues of the Sacred Heart, images and pictures started to disappear in a new generation of Catholics. Devotion to the Sacred Heart became a relic of the past, known and cherished only by a small minority of older Catholics.

Reflections and Conclusions

◇ The "devotion to the Sacred Heart" may disappear, but it must always be remembered that the heart is the most powerful human symbol that we have. If this disappears in regard to Christ, we are in danger of losing his humanity itself, which is at the central core of Christianity. One of the foremost theologians of our time, Karl Rahner, has taught and written about the necessity of images and symbols for our faith. In regard to the heart, he has explained that the heart of Christ is a necessary symbol for his human love; without it we are in danger of losing the essential nature of Christ's humanity. In his book, *Theological Investigations,* he wrote as follows, "This basic structure of all Christianity, which a theology of the symbol should investigate, is found once more in the devotion to the heart of Jesus, and is its perpetual justification."[41] A complete picture of Rahner's teaching in this area is found in the book by Annice Callahann, R.S.C.J., *Karl Rahner's Spirituality of the Pierced Heart: A Reinterpretation of Devotion to the Sacred Heart.*[42]

◇ While it is true St. Margaret Mary and others popularized devotion to the heart of Jesus, we have seen that they drew it from biblical roots, especially the Gospel of John. It is by no means a latecomer into the Christian faith.

◊ Christianity has its root in the loving death of Christ and its participatory celebration in baptism and the Eucharist. The earliest Christian writer, St. Paul, affirms that nothing in all of creation "will be able to separate us from the love of God in Christ Jesus" (Rom 8:30). This love of Christ finds its expression in his "obedience unto death" (Phil 2:8). While community emphasis is important, each individual must personally appreciate that love of Christ, and bring his/her life into conformity with it to live as a Christian. Here again, our greatest symbol and image of love is that of the heart. In the Eucharist, the celebration of the people of God must be accompanied by the offering of each person bringing his/her entire life in union with the offering of Christ on the cross. The morning offering in union with that of Christ's own heart was and remains a precious way of accepting all of life and its challenges while bringing them to the foot of the cross through each Mass. It is really nothing more than a practical application of the words of Paul, "Present your bodies as a living sacrifice, holy and acceptable to God, which is your spiritual worship" (Rom 12:1).

◊ Some of an older non-acceptable form of "reparation" crept into devotion to the heart of Christ through the revelations of Margaret Mary. In particular this meant "making up for" the hurts offered to his heart through the sins of the world. This was symbolized by the ring of thorns around his heart. But this does not mean that the essential core of worship and devotion to Christ's heart should be dropped.

◊ In addition, specific "guarantees" such as the Nine First

Fridays and the like must be rejected. Enough is Christ's assurance of love, and his promise that those who eat his flesh and drink his blood will always abide in him (Jn 6:53).

◊ It is good to keep in mind that each person must develop that form of heart image which is most appealing and helpful. St. Margaret Mary's vision of the burning wounded heart infused with light and surmounted by a cross was extremely helpful to herself and millions of others, but not to all. A good way to develop this is through meditation on the scriptural heart texts we have pointed out in this book. It was actually through this method that Margaret Mary, Gertrude, Teresa of Avila and others came to their own unique insights and images.

◊ Finally, the image of the Sacred Heart brought out an overwhelmingly sorrowful side of Christ. This sorrow was certainly present, as seen in Matthew's accounts of the Last Supper and agony in the garden where Jesus is grieved and heart-broken over the betrayals of Judas and Peter as well as the forthcoming desertion by his other disciples. However, the sorrow in Jesus' heart needs to be balanced by his predominant attitude of happiness and joy. This was felt and was manifest in the fun and laughter found in so many of his teachings and parables. This is especially reflected in the joyful tone in Luke's Gospel. I have tried to bring this out in a recent book called *God Makes Me Laugh: A New Approach to Luke*.[43]

12
Some New Directions in
Heart Imagery Applications[44]

The heart image is central not only to the Bible but to all human language and culture. In English, for example, the Oxford Dictionary of the English Language contains eighteen large columns devoted to various meanings of the heart, thus making it one of the most "loaded" words in the English language. In all there are fifty-six categories of meaning, with only four referring to the actual physical heart. The rest are by extension, metaphor or symbol. These metaphors or symbols are very important, for Ahsen's[45] research has shown that the metaphor is not just imagination but corresponds to an actual effect on the body. For example, to have a "broken heart" is not just figurative language but corresponds to a change in the physical organ. A heart specialist, Dr. Dean Orstein,[46] has found evidence that physical changes take place in the heart organ that correspond to heart language. For example, an unforgiving or "hardhearted" person actually brings about a corresponding "hardness" in the physical heart.

Therefore, the dictionary categories of meaning are important indicators of areas where heart symbolism will be effective in healing and personal integration. The following are the main headings under which the fifty-six categories are arranged: 1–4: the simple organ or function; 5–13: the seat of feeling, understanding and thought—e.g., to search the heart, open up one's heart, a merry, good or obstinate heart, to lose heart, or put one's heart into something; 14–16: the whole person—e.g., a dear heart, or a sweetheart; 17–19: a central position—the heart of a city, or the heart of a flower; 20–22: the vital part of principle—e.g., the heart of one's faith, or the heart of the land; 23–30: the shape of the heart; 31–39: prepositional phrases, such as "to learn by heart"; 40–48: together with a verb—e.g., to take to heart, or break one's heart; 49–53: with another noun; 54: proverbs; 55–56: attributive phrases and special combinations.

Looking to other cultures, we would have to trace the use of the heart image in literature, art, music, mythology and extra-biblical religions, but, to my knowledge, no thorough comprehensive study exists. The following are some limited examples. A history of the heart symbol in art would incorporate the ancient Egytian scene of the weighing of hearts on a balance in the great hall of judgment. Greek mythology would present the familiar scenes of Cupid with his bow and arrow piercing the hearts of men and women with his potions of love. For the Romans, the flaming heart was a well-known symbol of charity. Today, who does not know what it means to receive a big heart on a Valentine's Day card? The heart was widely used in healing and magic as outlined by A. Whitlock and also by M. Cavendish.[47] A study in depth on music and the heart would be most revealing, for our fascination with music goes back to the steady rhythm with endless variety that was experienced in the maternal heart beat in the womb.

In the Far East, ancient Hindu documents picture the heart as the innermost center of the human being, the place where God is found. In fact, they consider the very heart of the entire universe to be found in the human heart as the meeting place of the divine. In the Bhagavad Gita (about 100 A.D., but drawing from much earlier sources) we find the following: "The supreme Lord is situated in everyone's heart, O Arjuna, and is directing the wanderings of all living beings" (18:61). Also, "I am seated in everyone's heart and from me come remembrance, knowledge and forgetfulness" (15:15). Finally, "The universe is the cosmic form of the Universal Lord, and I am that Lord represented as their supersoul dwelling in the heart of every embodied being" (8:4).

Yet despite all this literature and background, it is surprising to see how relatively little attention has been given to the application of heart imagery until recent years. Assagioli stressed the importance of the human heart symbol in his approach to a personal process of integration in these words:

> A fruitful way to use this symbol is to ask the patient to visualize a huge heart, bigger than himself, and in this heart a door. Then ask the patient to open the door and to enter into the heart. What he finds there varies with each patient. But the actual use of this symbol as a technique reveals the importance of the ability of the therapist in handling it.[48]

A modern leader in the therapeutic use of the heart image has been Dr. Achter Ahsen. In his book *Psycheye,* he describes the Eidetic Parents Test. In this, the patient is directed to form an image of father and mother standing in front of him/her. The patient is told, "Imagine that a window has been carved in each chest and that you can see their hearts beating there . . . see their hearts beating, and describe how each parent's heart beats . . . is there any sign of anxiety in the heartbeats?"[49]

The therapist then directs the patient to write these down and gives him/her a set of steps and questions to bring out the full meaning of the experience. This is followed by analysis, concentration, and dialogue. Since the parental heartbeat, above all the mother's which began in the womb, is so primary in psychological development, the importance of this exercise as a basis for personal healing and integration can hardly be overemphasized. This is because the parental heart-beat and its influence go back to the earliest moments of existence in the womb and continue for months and sometimes years after birth. In addition, psychotherapy has brought out the central importance of accepting parents "as they are" as a first step in personal integration. The eidetic image of the beating heart constitutes a very effective way to bring about dramatic changes in this area.

I have worked with this image in a therapeutic environment with about twenty different people and have always been surprised by the results. Adapting Ahsen's process, I have utilized the following procedure: After relaxation exercises, I ask the persons to close their eyes and imagine that their mother (and later their father) is standing before them, and that a window is opened in each chest so they can see their parent's heart beating. They carefully note and describe this beat and detect whatever signs of joy or anxiety they find. Then they are asked in what way they wish the parental heart/heart beat to be different. This is to elicit the models or expectations in their mind that have caused their failure to accept their parents as they are. Next they focus on the suffering and disappointment in their own hearts that these demands, expectations and models of their parents have caused them. This step provides the opportunity to desire a change so they can be freed from this unnecessary suffering (since they have brought it on themselves by the models they themselves have created). The final step is that of complete acceptance: to listen to their parent's heart beat and completely accept it as it is, just as they accept their own heart beat.

Some actual examples taken from their own written summaries will illustrate the process more graphically:

1.   "I saw my mother's heart as beating rapidly with anxiety. I felt sorry for her. I took it into my heart and stroked it. Then I saw her heart as having hooks all around it, wanting to hook others into loving her continually. Then I realized I hadn't gotten in touch with my true feelings when my mother wanted to cling to me and not allow me to become an adult. The feelings of resentment and disappointment then came into consciousness. I was disappointed that I couldn't be free. Then I wondered why she had to be so 'clinging.' As I thought about it, I remembered her telling me that her own mother had died when she was ten and then she had a mean stepmother. My own dad was an alcoholic, so I figured she was desperate to have someone love her. It was a crying out from a long awaited need. That image of her desperate need for love helped me accept her as she was—a clinging mother."

2.   "I imagined my mother's heart, beating slowly and heavily, viewed through a window in her chest. It was very tired. I was not aware of any emotion or anxiety when viewing the heart movement from the outside. I found myself wishing her heart would show vitality, health and energy— not be weary. I wish she had been well and happy, for herself and other family members. I then focused on my own heart to experience the emotions more vividly. I became aware of the fear and desperation of a person whose perceptions of the other world were often distorted. She wished to be most good and perfect to and for everyone, and she felt she didn't

have a chance because of outside circumstances, or failure of others to do what she needed. What a tragedy! I became fatigued as a I resonated with her tired heart beat, and I accepted our heart beats as one. I accepted my mother as she was. I know she wished for health and vitality."

The exercise I have presented can also be done alone with fruitful results. It can also be extended to others close to us such as a spouse, friend or family member.

The following two examples are of special interest because they connect suffering and anxiety with a heart condition of the parent. This connection of stress and the heart is something we will take up shortly.

1. "My father was standing on the staircase looking down—very angry and yelling. His heart was beating rapidly, pounding and thumping. It looked like an anatomical heart. I had a difficult time focusing on anxiety, but finally decided there was anxiety beneath the anger. When I imagined this heart as my own, I could empathize—because I have felt this anger. When I made it my own, it became softer and slower. The anxiety was a fear of not being loved. My father had had a stroke and was very frustrated at not being able to live as he had before. I wished my father's heart were more loving and that he had not had a stroke. This demand did cause me to feel disappointment and sadness, perhaps also anger and fear. When I listened to his heart beat and accepted it as it was—my own heart beat—I knew that I am as he was! I understood his fear and frustration."

2. "My mother died of a heart attack when she was in her thirties. As the window was opened in her chest, I saw an oversized heart that beat in a slow, labored and anxious fashion. I saw the sorrowful, quiet face of my mother behind this

heart beat. My expectations and desires were that her heart would be more joyful and full of life, and this model made me sad. Then I tried to identify with her heart and feelings. Suddenly a chance remark of a relative came to my mind that hinted that my father had an affair with another woman, with whom he also had other children. I understood now that this was true, and that my mother was grieving over this infidelity and all it meant to our family. As I identified with my mother's heartbeat, I accepted the way she felt, and also accepted her early death of a 'broken heart.' "

The above two examples lead us to our next area of application in heart illness and healing symbols, especially metaphoric heart images. The effects of our high stress modern world on the human heart have been widely recognized. In a popular autobiographical novel, Norman Cousins[50] describes his experiences as a heart patient, the stressful causes of his illness, and the healing process of positive thinking, stress reduction, exercise and diet that brought him to recovery.

In a case-illustrated lecture before the Image Institute, Akhter Ahsen[51] has carefully illustrated how modern stress affects the heart. He noted that many heart attacks or palpitations occur during the night, in early morning, or after stressful work. This is because, during the work day, there is an unconscious pressure or constriction on the heart not to express itself in work-related activities, and thus its very beat is held back or limited. An effective therapy would provide means for the heart to express itself during work or business. The heart is a central organ that needs expression in ordinary situations; otherwise it will severely react through irregular beats, hypertension or other abnormalities, precisely because it is being so restrained in daily life. The heart needs to "open itself up" and relax through a thorough enjoyment of life and expression of emotions both at home and in the work-a-day world; sleep must be enjoyed along with play and work.

Because of the relationship of heart condition to emotional expression, Ahsen recommends more use of "tribal" and emotional language, which is heart-centered. This is why we gave so much attention at the beginning of this chapter to the Oxford Dictionary categories of heart meaning. The many metaphors of the heart actually respond to the physical heart condition and are a key to effective therapy when properly used. Of course it is a real challenge to begin a new "heart-centered" life style. The heart must be able to express in itself all the varying emotions—sadness, love, anger, bitterness, sweetness. It must be able to surrender itself to life rather than constrict itself, or withdraw from it.

An illustration of the effects of stress on the heart and the road to healing is provided by this excerpt of feedback from a patient after using the "open-heart" imagery (I almost wrote "surgery") described above:

"I pictured my father's chest exposed for my examination as he stands before me. His heart is misshapen and discolored from an old infarction. As I view his heart through the window, I sense that something is vitally wrong. His heart lacks a vital quality . . . I creep into his heart to experience it. To my surprise, it is filled with emotions—about people around him, his peers, acquaintances, family, and former wife (my mother). The emotions were mixed, positive and negative. They churn endlessly. Little, if any, of the emotion could be seen in his face. He did not know how to express it in a way that would not endanger him or his relationship with others. He could not trust enough to be open and share more tender feelings. I wish my father had expressed his emotions, and particularly the emotions of love, tenderness and fear which played a large part in his private life. Only in recent years did I make contact with these aspects. Most of our life, we were as aloof as strangers. My father and I are alike in many ways, and my reluctance to share 'vulnerable' emotions with others may represent his legacy."

The above experience shows the effects of suppression of the emotions on the heart. In the beginning of this chapter, we referred to the medical studies of heart specialist Dean Ornstein as confirming this and showing that heart-language actually does respond to physical heart conditions. The process also works in reverse—that new images of the heart can affect our language and behavior as well as our health. These can provide an impetus for a whole new way of living. The following are only some examples of the use of metamorphic heart images to bring about change.

Suggested Exercises

◊ We studied in Chapter 4 the Hebrew image of the listening heart and the example of King Solomon. After coming in contact with your heart beat in the way described in Chapters 2 and 3 close your eyes and pray like King Solomon for the gift of a listening heart. Focus your attention on your heart region, and come in contact with an image of your heart in your imagination. Imagine, according to the biblical view, the connection between heart and ears. Picture your heart as becoming more and more open and porous, literally "open-hearted," so that it is more and more sensitive to all of the impressions that come from the outside. Remember the biblical expression "the ears of the heart" and imagine that your heart is all covered with tiny ears that are open to other people's feelings and sensitive to the tiniest vibrations in the world around. Or imagine that these "ears" extend themselves like a TV antenna or satellite dish so they can be in tune with what has never before entered into your heart. Now focus on difficult areas in your life, personal relationships and work. Try to "hear with your heart" what is really going on. Then make appropriate decisions to bring more positive heart-language, expressions, feelings and bodily activity into these areas.

◊ "Healing the Heart" Each Evening
We often marvel how TV programs can be so perfectly executed, with exact timing, no mistakes, and the coordinated effort of such a large staff of skilled technicians and talented actors. But the secret is simple: they are not jittery or anxious; they know they can make mistakes and retape at any point. It is much the same way with the heart. We have tremendous healing powers within us, especially in the heart. As we look back on the day, we can feel discouraged or guilty, yet we can retape in such a way that the previous "failure" can become a tremendous success and learning experience. This is because everything we have done in the day is stored up in emotional packets in our memory, and these are accessible to us. We can discharge harmful and negative stored up energy, and replace it with positive, loving and dynamic impulses.

The way to do this is as follows: First of all imagine an incident where you have experienced negative or separating emotions such as anger, boredom, jealousy, hatred, etc. Go deeply into how you felt on this occasion, especially into your heart. Then allow these feelings to be expressed totally in yourself through "muscular discharge" or "catharsis." One helpful technique is to "breathe them in and out" until you feel they are discharged and you feel at peace. Sometimes this can be done in a few moments, but with traumatic experiences it may take more time, and the exercise may have to be repeated at intervals.

Once the "catharsis" or "erasing of tape" has been achieved, then the retaping can be done. Imagine the incident again, but go through it concentrating on the loving, compassionate side of your heart, and identifying with the feelings of others on this occasion. Accept the people and their feelings as if they were your own and forgive them. "Say" to them now what a loving and compassionate heart would have you say. Once this has happened, the whole event can be restored as a positive helpful memory in your life.

General Suggestions for the Optimum Use of Exercises in This Book

The manner of applying heart images is very important if we are to achieve their full dynamic possibilities. The following are some suggestions:

1. Their use should be sustained over a long period of time to overcome ingrained, emotionally-charged habits that have become part of daily life.

2. The deeper the state of relaxation, the easier it is for heart images to surface, and the more effective they will become. Spend some time in relaxing through breathing exercises before beginning. Assume an alert but comfortable position, and give sufficient time to the exercises.

3. A good time is early in the morning, so we can start the day with new energy and direction for the day's activities.

4. The image chosen should respond as closely as possible to the heart condition that needs remedy. A constricted, suppressed heart needs a corresponding remedial image of openness or broadness.

5. Although images work by their own inner power, they work much more quickly and effectively if we have confidence in their use.

6. Look upon mistakes and failures each day not as a loss but as a valuable learning experience. Everyone makes mistakes. The big difference is that some learn through them and some don't. That is why the "retaping" or "healing the heart" exercise each evening is so important and hopeful.

Notes

1. Samuels, p. 313
2. Jung, p. 252
3. pp. 17–19
4. As described by Samuels, pp. 226–227
5. p. 223
6. cf. bibliog.
7. cf. bibliog., Salk
8. cf. bibliog., de Chateau
9. cf. bibliog.,
10. cf. books of Cousins and Ornstein
11. Tape by Akhter Ahsen, bibliog.
12. cf. bibliog., Hertz, p. 119
13. The historical development of ethical meaning in the term "Spirit" is surveyed in the article by R.J. Sklba.
14. p. 494
15. Probhavananda, p. 49
16. esp. pp. 5–12
17. p. 210
18. p. 227
19. The sense of identification that Paul felt with Christ is a central theme in my book, *The Secret of Paul the Apostle.*
20. cf. bibliog.
21. cf. bibliog.
22. p. 275

23. A detailed study of the special place of Jesus' mother in the fourth gospel is found in my article, "The Role of Jesus' Mother in John's Gospel."

24. cf. bibliog.

25. pp.285–294

26. *In Joannis Evangelium*, P.L. XXV, 1536. The citations of the writers in this chapter are from Williams.

27. *Historia Ecclesiastica*, V,1

28. *In Joannem*, P.G. XIV, 808

29. *Exposition Super Canticam*, P.L. LXXIX, 499

30. *In Canticam*, P.L. XCI, 1139

31. *Meditatio* X, P.L. CLVIII, 761

32. *Sermo in Canticis*, LXI, P.L.CLXXXIII, 1070

33. *De Emmanuele*, P.L. CXCVI, 655

34. Williams, p. 47

35. from the *Life and Revelations of St. Gertrude*, (Burns, 1970) pp. 184–190. Cf. Williams, p. 53

36. Williams, p. 59

37. Thomas Hemerken a Kempis, *Opera Omnia*, (Freibourg, 1910) Vol. III, p. 197, cf. Williams, p. 85

38. *Oeuvres de Saint Francois de Sales*, (Annecy, 1908) from Williams, p. 96

39. Hamon, A., *Histoire de la Devotion au Sacre Coeur*, 5 vols., (Paris, 1923–39) Vol. 1, p. 140. Taken from Williams, pp. 15–16

40. Hamon, *op. cit*, p. 173.

41. pp. 221–252

42. cf. bibliog.

43. cf. bibliog.

44. This chapter is adapted from an article entitled, "Heart Imagery: Some New Directions in Healing and Psychotherapeutic Applications," Scheduled for publication in the *Journal of Mental Imagery*.

45. cf. bibliog.

46. cf. bibliog.

47. cf. bibliog., Maple's article is in M. Cavendish's book.

48. *Psychosynthesis*, p. 187
49. *Psycheye*, p. 236
50. cf. bibliog.
51. cf. note 45

Bibliography
Books and Articles Consulted

Ahsen, Akhter, "The Imagery Treatment of Hypertension and Heart Problems," Cassette #19. Tape available from *Pro-Helios,* Yonkers, N.Y. 1983

Ahsen, A., *Psycheye* (N.Y.: Brandon House, 1977)

Assagioli, R., *Psychosynthesis* (N.Y.: Viking, 1965)

———*The Act of the Will* (N.Y.: Viking, 1973)

Betz, O., *Galatians* (Phila.: Westminster, 1975)

Brown, R.E., *The Gospel According to John (i–xii)* (Garden City, N.Y.: Doubleday, 1966)

Callahan, Annice, *Karl Rahner's Spirituality of the Pierced Heart: A Reinterpretation of Devotion to the Sacred Heart* (Lanham, Md.: University of America Press, 1985)

Cavandish, M. (ed.), *Man, Myth, & Magic,* under "Heart," by E. Maple (N.Y.: M. Cavendish Corp., 1983)

Cousins, Norman, *The Healing Heart* (N.Y.: Norton, 1983)

DeChateau, P., Holmberg, H., Winberg, J., "Left Side Preference in Holding and Carrying New-Born Infants" (*Acta Paediatrica Scandinavica* 67 (1978) pp. 169–175

Eichdrodt, W., *Ezekiel* (Phila.: Westminster, 1975)

Ellis, P., *The Genius of John* (Collegeville, Minn.: Liturgical Press, 1984)

Gerhardsson, B., *The Ethos of the Bible,* trans. S. Westerholm (Phila.: Fortress, 1981)

Girard, M., "La Composition Structurelle des Sept Signes dans le Quatrième Evangile," *Sciences Réligeuses* 9(1980) pp. 315–324

Grassi, J., "The Role of Jesus' Mother in John's Gospel: A Reappraisal," (scheduled for the Jan. 1986 *Catholic Biblical Quarterly*)

———, *God Makes Me Laugh: A New Approach to Luke* (Wilmington, Del: M. Glazier, 1985)

———, *The Secret of Paul the Apostle* (Maryknoll, N.Y.: Orbis, 1978)

Hertz, Joseph, *The Authorized Daily Prayer Book* (N.Y.: Bloch, 1948)

Jung, C., *Memories, Dreams, Reflections* (N.Y.: Vintage Books, 1963)

Kasemann, E., *Commentary on Romans,* trans., ed., G.W. Bromily (Grand Rapids: Eerdmans, 1980)

Kim, S., *The Origin of Paul's Gospel* (Grand Rapids: Eerdmans, 1982)

Milgrom, Jo, "When Is a Heart Not a Heart? A Search for Primary Meanings of Heart Images in the Hebrew Bible." (Unpublished manuscript)

Minear, P., "The Beloved Disciple in the Gospel of John: Some Clues and Conjectures," *Novum Testamentum* 19 (1977) pp. 105–123

Ornish, Dean, *Stress, Diet and Your Heart* (N.Y.: Signet Books, 1982)

Probhavananda & Isherwood, *How To Know God: The Yoga Aphorisms of Patanjali* (N.Y.: New American Library, 1952)

Rahner, K., *Theological Investigations* (N.Y.: Seabury, 1974)

Salk, L., "The Role of the Heartbeat in the Relationship Between Mother and Infant," *Scientific American* 228(1973) pp. 24–29

Samuels, M. & N., *Seeing With The Mind's Eye: The History, Techniques and Use of Visualization* (N.Y.: Random House, 1975)

Sklba, R.J., "Until the Spirit from On High Is Poured Out on Us," *Catholic Biblical Quarterly* 46 (1984) pp. 1–17

Whitlock, A., *Symbols, Signs and Their Meaning* (Newton: C.T. Bradford, 1961)

Williams, M., *The Sacred Heart in the Life of the Church* (N.Y.: Sheed & Ward, 1957)